SUDAN

SUDAN

1880 TO THE PRESENT:
CROSSROADS OF A CONTINENT IN CONFLICT

DANIEL E. HARMON

INTRODUCTORY ESSAY BY
Dr. Richard E. Leakey
Chairman, Wildlife Clubs
of Kenya Association
✝
AFTERWORD BY
Deirdre Shields

CHELSEA HOUSE PUBLISHERS
Philadelphia
In association with Covos Day Books, South Africa

CHELSEA HOUSE PUBLISHERS

EDITOR IN CHIEF Sally Cheney
PRODUCTION MANAGER Pamela Loos
ART DIRECTOR Sara Davis
PICTURE EDITOR Judy L. Hasday
MANAGING EDITOR James D. Gallagher
SENIOR PRODUCTION EDITOR LeeAnne Gelletly
ASSOCIATE ART DIRECTOR Takeshi Takahashi
SERIES DESIGNER Keith Trego
COVER DESIGN Emiliano Begnardi

The Chelsea House World Wide Web address is http://www.chelseahouse.com

First Printing
1 3 5 7 9 8 6 4 2

Library of Congress Cataloging-in-Publication Data

Harmon, Daniel E.
    Sudan / Daniel E. Harmon.
            p. cm. — (Exploration of Africa)
    Includes bibliographical references and index.
    ISBN 0-7910-5453-5 (hardcover)
      1. Sudan—History—Juvenile literature. [1. Sudan—History.] I. Title.
    II. Exploration of Africa, the emerging nations.

DT155.6 .H365 2000
962.4—dc21
                                                            00-059638

The photographs in this book are from the Royal Geographical Society Picture Library. Most are being published for the first time.

The Royal Geographical Society Picture Library provides an unrivaled source of over half a million images of peoples and landscapes from around the globe. Photographs date from the 1840s onwards on a variety of subjects including the British Colonial Empire, deserts, exploration, indigenous peoples, landscapes, remote destinations, and travel.

Photography, beginning with the daguerreotype in 1839, is only marginally younger than the Society, which encouraged its explorers to use the new medium from its earliest days. From the remarkable mid-19th century black-and-white photographs to color transparencies of the late 20th century, the focus of the collection is not the generic stock shot but the portrayal of man's resilience, adaptability, and mobility in remote parts of the world.

In organizing this project, we have incurred many debts of gratitude. Our first, though, is to the professional staff of the Picture Library for their generous assistance, especially to Joanna Scadden, Picture Library Manager.

CONTENTS

Exploration of Africa: The Emerging Nations

THE DARK CONTINENT

DR. RICHARD E. LEAKEY

THE CONCEPT OF AFRICAN exploration has been greatly influenced by the hero status given to the European adventurers and missionaries who went off to Africa in the last century. Their travels and travails were certainly extraordinary and nobody can help but be impressed by the tremendous physical and intellectual courage that was so much a characteristic of people such as Livingstone, Stanley, Speke, and Baker, to name just a few. The challenges and rewards that Africa offered, both in terms of commerce and also "saved souls," inspired people to take incredible risks and endure personal suffering to a degree that was probably unique to the exploration of Africa.

I myself was fortunate enough to have had the opportunity to organize one or two minor expeditions to remote spots in Africa where there were no roads or airfields and marching with porters and/or camels was the best option at the time. I have also had the thrill of being with people untouched and often unmoved by contact with Western or other technologically based cultures, and these experiences remain for me amongst the most exciting and salutary of my life. With the contemporary revolution in technology, there will be few if any such opportunities again. Indeed I often find myself slightly saddened by the realization that were life ever discovered on another planet, exploration would doubtless be done by remote sensing and making full use of artificial, digital intelligence. At least it is unlikely to be in my lifetime and this is a relief!

INTRODUCTION

Notwithstanding all of this, I believe that the age of exploration and discovery in Africa is far from over. The future offers incredible opportunities for new discoveries that will push back the frontiers of knowledge. This endeavor will of course not involve exotic and arduous journeys into malaria-infested tropical swamps, but it will certainly require dedication, team work, public support, and a conviction that the rewards to be gained will more than justify the efforts and investment.

EARLY EXPLORERS

Many of us were raised and educated at school with the belief that Africa, the so-called Dark Continent, was actually discovered by early European travelers and explorers. The date of this "discovery" is difficult to establish, and anyway a distinction has always had to be drawn between northern Africa and the vast area south of the Sahara. The Romans certainly had information about the continent's interior as did others such as the Greeks. A diverse range of traders ventured down both the west coast and the east coast from at least the ninth century, and by the tenth century Islam had taken root in a number of new towns and settlements established by Persian and Arab interests along the eastern tropical shores. Trans-African trade was probably under way well before this time, perhaps partly stimulated by external interests.

Close to the beginning of the first millennium, early Christians were establishing the Coptic church in the ancient kingdom of Ethiopia and at other coastal settlements along Africa's northern Mediterranean coast. Along the west coast of Africa, European trade in gold, ivory, and people was well established by the sixteenth century. Several hundred years later, early in the 19th century, the systematic penetration and geographical exploration of Africa was undertaken by Europeans seeking geographical knowledge and territory and looking for opportunities not only for commerce but for the chance to spread the Gospel. The extraordinary narratives of some of the journeys of early European travelers and adventurers in Africa are a vivid reminder of just how recently Africa has become embroiled in the power struggles and vested interests of non-Africans.

THE DARK CONTINENT

AFRICA'S GIFT TO THE WORLD

My own preoccupation over the past thirty years has been to study human prehistory, and from this perspective it is very clear that Africa was never "discovered" in the sense in which so many people have been and, perhaps, still are being taught. Rather, it was Africans themselves who found that there was a world beyond their shores.

Prior to about two million years ago, the only humans or proto-humans in existence were confined to Africa; as yet, the remaining world had not been exposed to this strange mammalian species, which in time came to dominate the entire planet. It is no trivial matter to recognize the cultural implications that arise from this entirely different perspective of Africa and its relationship to the rest of humanity.

How many of the world's population grow up knowing that it was in fact African people who first moved and settled in southern Europe and Central Asia and migrated to the Far East? How many know that Africa's principal contribution to the world is in fact humanity itself? These concepts are quite different from the notion that Africa was only "discovered" in the past few hundred years and will surely change the commonly held idea that somehow Africa is a "laggard," late to come onto the world stage.

It could be argued that our early human forebears—the *Homo erectus* who moved out of Africa—have little or no bearing on the contemporary world and its problems. I disagree and believe that the often pejorative thoughts that are associated with the Dark Continent and dark skins, as well as with the general sense that Africans are somehow outside the mainstream of human achievement, would be entirely negated by the full acceptance of a universal African heritage for all of humanity. This, after all, is the truth that has now been firmly established by scientific inquiry.

The study of human origins and prehistory will surely continue to be important in a number of regions of Africa and this research must continue to rank high on the list of relevant ongoing exploration and discovery. There is still much to be learned about the early stages of human development, and the age of the "first humans"—the first bipedal apes—has not been firmly established. The current hypothesis is that prior to five million years ago there were no bipeds, and this would mean that humankind is only five million years old. Beyond Africa, there were no humans until just two million years ago, and this is a consideration that political leaders and people as a whole need to bear in mind.

RECENT HISTORY

When it comes to the relatively recent history of Africa's contemporary people, there is still considerable ignorance. The evidence suggests that there were major migrations of people within the continent during the past 5,000 years, and the impact of the introduction of domestic stock must have been quite considerable on the way of life of many of Africa's people. Early settlements and the beginnings of nation states are, as yet, poorly researched and recorded. Although archaeological studies have been undertaken in Africa for well over a hundred years, there remain more questions than answers.

One question of universal interest concerns the origin and inspiration for the civilization of early Egypt. The Nile has, of course, offered opportunities for contacts between the heart of Africa and the Mediterranean seacoast, but very little is known about human settlement and civilization in the upper reaches of the Blue and White Nile between 4,000 and 10,000 years ago. We do know that the present Sahara Desert is only about 10,000 years old; before this Central Africa was wetter and more fertile, and research findings have shown that it was only during the past 10,000 years that Lake Turkana in the northern Kenya was isolated from the Nile system. When connected, it would have been an excellent connection between the heartland of the continent and the Mediterranean.

Another question focuses on the extensive stone-walled villages and towns in Southern Africa. The Great Zimbabwe is but one of thousands of standing monuments in East, Central, and Southern Africa that attest to considerable human endeavor in Africa long before contact with Europe or Arabia. The Neolithic period and Iron Age still offer very great opportunities for exploration and discovery.

As an example of the importance of history, let us look at the modern South Africa where a visitor might still be struck by the not-too-subtle representation of a past that, until a few years ago, only "began" with the arrival of Dutch settlers some 400 years back. There are, of course, many pre-Dutch sites, including extensive fortified towns where kingdoms and nation states had thrived hundreds of years before contact with Europe; but this evidence has been poorly documented and even more poorly portrayed.

Few need to be reminded of the sparseness of Africa's precolonial written history. There are countless cultures and historical narratives that have been recorded only as oral history and legend. As postcolonial Africa further consolidates itself, history must be reviewed and deepened to incorporate the realities of precolonial human settlement as well as foreign contact. Africa's identity and self-respect is closely linked to this.

One of the great tragedies is that African history was of little interest to the early European travelers who were in a hurry and had no brief to document the details of the people they came across during their travels. In the basements of countless European museums, there are stacked shelves of African "curios"—objects taken from the people but seldom documented in terms of the objects' use, customs, and history.

There is surely an opportunity here for contemporary scholars to do something. While much of Africa's precolonial past has been obscured by the slave trade, colonialism, evangelism, and modernization, there remains an opportunity, at least in some parts of the continent, to record what still exists. This has to be one of the most vital frontiers for African exploration and discovery as we approach the end of this millennium. Some of the work will require trips to the field, but great gains could be achieved by a systematic and coordinated effort to record the inventories of European museums and archives. The Royal Geographical Society could well play a leading role in this chapter of African exploration. The compilation of a central data bank on what is known and what exists would, if based on a coordinated initiative to record the customs and social organization of Africa's remaining indigenous peoples, be a huge contribution to the heritage of humankind.

MEDICINES AND FOODS

On the African continent itself, there remain countless other areas for exploration and discovery. Such endeavors will be achieved without the fanfare of great expeditions and high adventure as was the case during the last century and they should, as far as possible, involve exploration and discovery of African frontiers by Africans themselves. These frontiers are not geographic: they are boundaries of knowledge in the sphere of Africa's home-grown cultures and natural world.

Indigenous knowledge is a very poorly documented subject in many parts of the world, and Africa is a prime example of a continent where centuries of accumulated local knowledge is rapidly disappearing in the face of modernization. I believe, for example, that there is much to be learned about the use of wild African plants for both medicinal and nutritional purposes. Such knowledge, kept to a large extent as the experience and memory of elders in various indigenous communities, could potentially have far-reaching benefits for Africa and for humanity as a whole.

The importance of new remedies based on age-old medicines cannot be underestimated. Over the past two decades, international companies have begun to take note and to exploit certain African plants for pharmacological preparations. All too often, Africa has not been the beneficiary of these "discoveries," which are, in most instances, nothing more than the refinement and improvement of traditional African medicine. The opportunities for exploration and discovery in this area are immense and will have assured economic return on investment. One can only hope that such work will be in partnership with the people of Africa and not at the expense of the continent's best interests.

Within the same context, there is much to be learned about the traditional knowledge of the thousands of plants that have been utilized by different African communities for food. The contemporary world has become almost entirely dependent, in terms of staple foods, on the cultivation of only six principal plants: corn, wheat, rice, yams, potatoes, and bananas. This cannot be a secure basis to guarantee the food requirements of more than five billion people.

Many traditional food plants in Africa are drought resistant and might well offer new alternatives for large-scale agricultural development in the years to come. Crucial to this development is finding out what African people used before exotics were introduced. In some rural areas of the continent, it is still possible to learn about much of this by talking to the older generation. It is certainly a great shame that some of the early European travelers in Africa were ill equipped to study and record details of diet and traditional plant use, but I am sure that, although it is late, it is not too late. The compilation of a pan-African database on what is known about the use of the continent's plant resources is a vital matter requiring action.

VANISHING SPECIES

In the same spirit, there is as yet a very incomplete inventory of the continent's other species. The inevitable trend of bringing land into productive management is resulting in the loss of unknown but undoubtedly large numbers of species. This genetic resource may be invaluable to the future of Africa and indeed humankind, and there really is a need for coordinated efforts to record and understand the continent's biodiversity.

In recent years important advances have been made in the study of tropical ecosystems in Central and South America, and I am sure that similar endeavors in Africa would be rewarding. At present, Africa's semi-arid and highland ecosystems are better understood than the more diverse and complex lowland forests, which are themselves under particular threat from loggers and farmers. The challenges of exploring the biodiversity of the upper canopy in the tropical forests, using the same techniques that are now used in Central American forests, are fantastic and might also lead to eco-tourist developments for these areas in the future.

It is indeed an irony that huge amounts of money are being spent by the advanced nations in an effort to discover life beyond our own planet, while at the same time nobody on this planet knows the extent and variety of life here at home. The tropics are especially relevant in this regard and one can only hope that Africa will become the focus of renewed efforts of research on biodiversity and tropical ecology.

AN AFROCENTRIC VIEW

Overall, the history of Africa has been presented from an entirely Eurocentric or even Caucasocentric perspective, and until recently this has not been adequately reviewed. The penetration of Africa, especially during the last century, was important in its own way; but today the realities of African history, art, culture, and politics are better known. The time has come to regard African history in terms of what has happened in Africa itself, rather than simply in terms of what non-African individuals did when they first traveled to the continent.

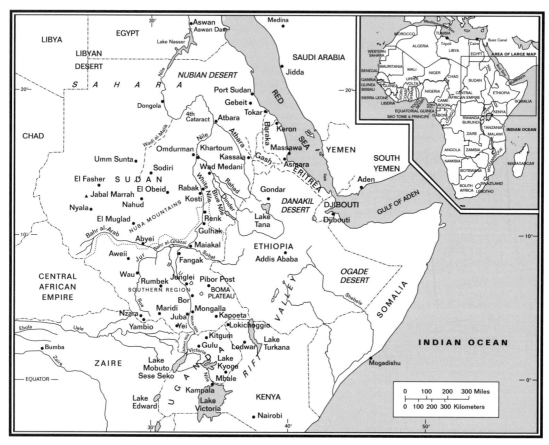

The Republic of Sudan, the largest African nation.

INTRODUCTION

It was a rare encounter: two parties of British explorers, one bedraggled after two years in the wild but with exciting news to tell, one recently embarked on a new adventure. They met on a mighty, mystical river, surrounded by a vast unknown. The year was 1862. The place: Gondokoro, near the headwaters of the White Nile.

Northbound toward the Mediterranean Sea were John Hanning Speke and James Augustus Grant. They had left England in 1860, determined to prove Lake Victoria at the equator was the source of the great Nile. Speke, only in his mid-thirties, had been there before, tracking along an overland Arab trading route. He was the first European in history to view the lake, second largest in the world, which he named after his queen. His latest findings, which would not be verified for several years, demonstrated that the lake was indeed the primary source of the White Nile.

Southbound from Cairo, Egypt, was Samuel Baker. In his early forties, Baker had earned a name as an explorer and colonial settler in Ceylon, the great island off the southern tip of India. Traveling now with the adventuress Florence von Sass (his future wife), he had the same ambition as Speke and Grant: to identify the source of the Nile.

The Nile . . . for centuries a ribbon of life through barren lands. Ancient Greek and Roman conquerors marveled at the beauty of its fertile delta, the center of Egyptian civilization. Napoleon Bonaparte tried to colonize the delta and sent scholars upriver to investigate the timeless treasures of Egypt.

Further south the Nile valley became less hospitable to European visitors. The river disappeared through a desert; split; watered a curious, humid swampland; and meandered through green hills teeming with wildlife where lay its source—or sources—unknown. Hundreds of miles of the alluring watercourse and its tributaries awaited the probes of white explorers.

Ancient Egyptians undoubtedly had traveled the river beyond the fork of the White and Blue Niles. There is no indication, however, that they ever traced those branches to their sources. Nor had the Greeks or Romans—although Emperor Nero sent a Roman expedition upriver in A.D. 66; the Romans were blocked by swamplands in what is today southern Sudan. To chart the Nile became a major objective of nineteenth-century geographers, particularly those in Great Britain.

Population: more than 31 million

Area: 967,243 square miles

Capital: Khartoum

Primary language: Arabic

Neighboring countries/body of water: Egypt, Libya, Chad, Central African Republic, Congo, Uganda, Kenya, Ethiopia, Eritrea, Red Sea

Highest point: Mt. Kinyeti, 10,456 feet

Major economic activity: agriculture

Main unit of currency: the *dinar*

Flag: bright green triangle pointing inward from the left edge; three horizontal bars extending from it to the right edge (red on top, white in the middle, black on the bottom)

INTRODUCTION

The English explorers in 1862 parted with what undoubtedly were mixed emotions on both sides. Had Speke and Grant definitely beaten him to his goal, Baker must have wondered, or was the true source of the Nile yet to be found? The idea of Lake Victoria feeding the river was a subject of lively debate among geographers at the time. Baker himself would explore additional terrain around the headwaters of the White Nile and other rivers.

For their part, the returning veterans, while confident in their own work, surely wondered whether Baker might undermine their triumph by locating another lake, perhaps a larger one!

The story of the exploration and development of the Nile is in large part the story of Sudan. Today the importance of Sudan among the emerging African nations stems primarily from the grand river that traverses it. In this book we will examine the people of Sudan, the river, and the cast of characters—including Samuel Baker—who have carved the path of the country into the modern era. It's a story fraught with struggle and tragedy, yet filled with excitement and rich with a wonderful mixture of African cultures.

The Palace, Khartoum, 1899 *This shell of a building was what remained of Khartoum after al-Mahdi's siege of the capital of the Sudan (March 13, 1884–January 26, 1885). From this white-walled palace, out of its louvered windows, one could see the shimmer of the Blue Nile and, in the distance, the majestic sight of the White Nile joining forces with the Blue.*

In early 1884, following a series of Mahdist victories in the Egyptian-ruled Sudan, the British government reluctantly sent General Charles Gordon to evacuate the Egyptian garrison from Khartoum. Gordon reached the capital on February 18, 1884, and succeeded in evacuating some 2,000 women and children before the Mahdi forces closed in on the city. Gordon refused to retreat. Although the British government eventually sent a relief force, it was too late. The siege of Khartoum ended with the Mahdi's capture of the city and the massacre of its defenders, including Gordon. Except for the principal mosque, the city was totally destroyed. Al-Mahdi set up his capital across the Nile at Omdurman. Reoccupied in 1898, Khartoum was rebuilt by Major General Kitchener. The city served as the seat of the Anglo-Egyptian Sudan government until 1956, when it became the capital of the independent Sudan.

THE LAY OF THE LAND

Foreigners who visit Africa are awed by its vastness. It is, after all, the second largest of Earth's five continents. And the largest African nation on the face of this great continent is the Republic of the Sudan—almost 1 million square miles (more than one-and-a-half times the size of Alaska).

It is difficult mentally to grasp such a piece of geography. Sudan challenges our understanding not just because of its enormity but because of the dramatic geographic differences we find from border to border. Deserts in the east and west flank the River Nile valley that extends down the center of the country. Ethiopian and Eritrean highlands line the eastern fringe. Grass-covered plains cross the central landscape. As we move southward and southwestward from the sudd swamps of the upper Nile near Sudan's southern border, approaching the river's headwaters, we enter the equatorial heart of Africa with its breathtaking variety of jungle vegetation and wildlife.

When studying northern Africa, it is important to distinguish between the Republic of the Sudan (the nation that is the subject of this book) and the much broader geographic region known as "the Sudan." The Republic of the Sudan, directly south of Egypt, is the largest country on the African continent. The Sudan region encompasses much more territory than the republic. It spans the continent of Africa south of the Sahara Desert and north of the central rainforests, all the way from the Red Sea in the northeast to the Atlantic Ocean in the west. When the European nations "partitioned" the African continent in the late 1800s, one large area was known to them as French Sudan. This was on the Atlantic coast—on the other side of the continent from the modern Republic of the Sudan!

In this book, we'll discuss some general characteristics of the Sudan region but focus on the specific history and development of the Republic of the Sudan. For convenience, we will refer to the country as simply "Sudan." An ancient Arabic translation of the term "Sudan" is "land of the black peoples."

HEART OF THE NILE

Dry, scorching heat and shifting, wind-whipped sand made travel and trade from Egypt down through the desert into Sudan difficult and dismal. It took weeks or months. One camel route extended from Asyut, a River Nile port in central Egypt, to El Fasher in the Darfur province of western Sudan. It consisted of a series of links from one isolated water well or oasis to another. In addition to the goods they were transporting, caravaners had to carry along heavy stores of drinking water. This desert trip took six weeks.

Naturally, many traders preferred passage along the River Nile. But this route entailed hardships of its own, as we will see.

The Nile is the longest river in the world. From its headwaters on the East African Plateau, it flows from south to north more than 4,000 miles. It empties into the Mediterranean Sea in northern Egypt. The fertile Nile basin—the main river plus the network of rivers and streams that empty into it—with its irrigation systems covers 10 percent of the African continent. The Nile cuts through the entire length of both Egypt and Sudan. Most of the two countries' populations live near the river.

John Hanning Speke's Lake Victoria—bordered by Kenya, Tanzania, and Uganda—marks the origin of the White Nile, more than 2,000 miles south of Khartoum, the Sudanese capital. The Blue Nile begins about 900 miles from Khartoum near Lake Tana in Ethiopia, Sudan's neighbor to the east.

In ages past, the Nile was considered a god. It is so long that no single tribe of ancient people knew its scope from source to delta. As late as the 1960s, mountain gorges near the head of the Blue Nile were still being mapped.

Because the river flows northward, discussions of the Nile may seem backward. When we speak of the "lower Nile," we are not talking about its southern reaches, as you might expect if you're looking at it on a globe. Rather, we are referring to its main course northward through Egypt, fanning out into its delta mouth and emptying into the Mediterranean Sea. If you are traveling "down the Nile" (with the current), you are traveling generally northward. The "upper Nile," on the other hand, refers to the southern branches of the river, moving upstream (southward or eastward) along the White and Blue Niles toward their headwaters in the east African interior.

Changing Landscapes

Moving up the Nile (southward) from Aswan in Egypt, we encounter a series of cataracts between Aswan and the Sudan capital of Khartoum. These waterfalls and rapids marked by sharp granite rocks, often impassable, total six in number and mark a distance of approximately 1,000 miles of river.

Author Mekki Abbas, in his book *The Sudan Question,* described the navigational hazards posed by the cataracts: "It is almost possible for a man, when the river is low, to get across by jumping from rock to rock. During the three months when the river is high the rocks are not visible, but they are so near the surface that even sailing boats cannot go over the cataract area without running serious risks."

The river cataracts and the difficulties of caravan travel through the hot desert sands have combined for thousands of years to frustrate passage between Egypt and Sudan. The problem changed little until rail lines were completed in northern Sudan during the late nineteenth century from Egypt and from Port Sudan on the Red Sea coast in the northeast.

The first cataract was the site chosen for building the Aswan dams. The idea of damming the mighty Nile to help control the region's water supply goes back more than a century. The original Aswan Dam was the river's first. It was built in 1902 and enlarged during the 1930s. In 1960 the Egyptians began constructing a new dam, the Aswan High Dam. It took eight years to build, at a cost of more than $1 billion. The Aswan High Dam created a major lake, named Lake Nasser after Egypt's first president. One of the largest lakes in Africa, it is 10 miles wide and 300 miles long, reaching southwestward all the way to the Sudan border.

Elephantine Island, a Nile landmark just below the first cataract, traditionally was considered the "door" between ancient Egyptian cultures and those of Nubia, Sudan, and the African interior. The Egyptian pharaohs installed a lineage of nobility on the isle, charging them with protecting Egypt from southern invasions. Ancient papyri indicate Elephantine was an important military outpost many centuries before the Christian era. The Elephantine rulers kept large armies whose warriors included the Medjai people, native herdsmen.

For several hundred miles below the Egyptian border, the Nile is flanked by desert. Here the summer temperature can exceed 125 degrees Fahrenheit. In the vicinity of Karima, we begin to see palm trees and other greenery. People in the remote areas of the north live in mud-brick, rectangular houses.

When we pass Khartoum in north-central Sudan, the land between the Blue and White Nile rivers opens into rich fields of cotton, grain, and other crops. Cotton and cottonseed from this region became important staples of Sudan's twentieth-century economy after dams were built and irrigation systems were developed.

Elsewhere across central Sudan, the land is a broad plain, or savanna, covered by grass and shrubs. On the western side of the White Nile, toward the Kordofan hill country, fields of millet and other crops surround villages of straw huts. Further south, with increased rainfall, the country is thicker and greener with grass and trees. The land here is especially good for farming and for raising cattle for sale at market.

Interestingly, although we are drawing nearer the equator as we travel southward, the average temperatures fall markedly. That's because we are leaving the dry, sandy eastern Sahara.

In its upper branches to the south, the Nile environment changes even more. We enter a flood plain, much of it jungle or mountain forest. Annual rainfall, which averages perhaps 4 inches in the northern Sudanese desert and 12 inches around Khartoum, in some years tops 50 inches at the country's southern border. Animal life, including big game, and bird life abound. The terrain ranges from savannas along the Blue Nile to rich forests. Here, the means of livelihood is not restricted by climate and geography; different people fish, farm, and graze livestock.

River of Grass: The Sudd Swamp

A drastic—and problematic—alteration is seen on the White Nile in the area of Juba, a southern Sudanese city near the Uganda/Zaire border. Water grass floats along the White Nile banks. As we continue upstream, this grassy periphery encroaches gradually into the waterway. The river divides into a maze of channels and becomes a shallow, vast, reed-choked swamp. Thick, tough-trunked, flowering reeds grow as high as 20 feet! The swamp also contains great quantities of papyrus, a type of reed that was used in making ancient paper.

These sudd swamps stymied the travels upriver of early European explorers. Englishman Sir Samuel Baker, the veteran explorer we met in our introduction, returned to the upper Nile to put down the slave trade in 1869. His diary is agonizing to read. One entry:

> Made about 300 yards of heavy cutting through rafts [floating masses] of vegetation. The lake of last year nearly choked up; about 100 acres of rafts having completely destroyed it.

Southern Sudan.

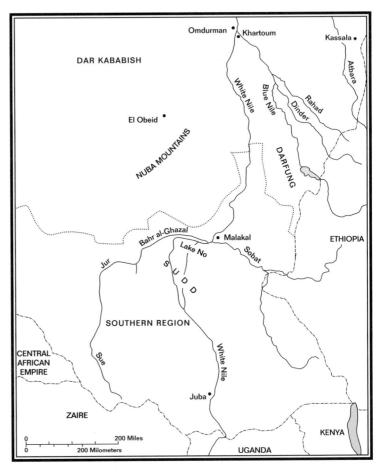

Baker spoke of "distressing shallows" (water only two to three feet deep—hardly ample to float a cargo-laden steamship) and "horrible chaos, which changes its appearance constantly." His men had to throw supplies overboard to lighten the vessels. His entry of February 8, 1870:

> This is the date of departure last year from Khartoum; in inconceivable madness, had any one known the character of the river. All hands as usual tugging, hauling, and deepening the river with spades and hoes; but the more we dig, the faster the water runs out of the bed, which threatens to leave us high and dry.

Later, river voyagers began using dynamite to open the sudd channels for steamers and other heavy boats.

Another problem with the sudd region is that much of the upper Nile's water—millions of cubic yards each year—simply evaporates here. A 224-mile canal presently is being dug around the swampland. It is hoped to save at least a fraction of the lost volume of the upper Nile.

A positive feature of the sudd swampland is its ecosystem of constant natural moisture for the surrounding region. The greenery easily supports livestock. Annual rainfall is about 60 inches. (Khartoum, some 600 miles north, typically must weather drought conditions more than half the year.)

Harnessing a Great River

The Nile for ages has been vital for its irrigation. People of the valley have found ways to spread the river waters outward many miles to irrigate their croplands. Beginning in the twentieth century, the river also was used to generate power. Dams at Sennar and Roseires on the Blue Nile are responsible for four-fifths of Sudan's electric power. Meanwhile, they make it possible to irrigate several thousand square miles of cotton fields in the Gezira region between the White and Blue Niles.

Natives even today use the Nile for trade. Many goods are carried in feluccas, which are boats driven by large, triangular sails, supplemented by oars. The Nile has been the region's main "highway" since early times. Drawings made thousands of years ago depict freight boats and ships of royal parties, some with sails, plying the Nile.

In the late 1800s the Europeans launched steamboats on the Nile and other African rivers. Steamers became important to both the Europeans and the natives for transporting people and commerce between river and ocean ports and the continent's interior. Some of these steamers served into the middle and late twentieth century.

The damming of the Nile and the creation of lakes upstream, while important to agricultural development, has alarmed

Native Boat, Sobat River, 1899 *The Sobat River is a major Sudanese tributary of the Nile, joining it at Malakal to form the White Nile. The Sobat carries a whitish sediment that gives the White Nile its name. During the dry season, the lowering of the river level uncovers land that cattle-owning people of the region use for grazing. This photograph was taken by Captain M. S. Wellby (1866–1900). Wellby, one of the most promising of a younger generation of explorers, was killed during the South African War. Wellby's principle geographic explorations occurred in Tibet.* Through Unknown Tibet, *his published account of his adventures, received extensive coverage in the popular press. His last exploration trip, which took seven months, was to Ethiopia—and then to find the source of the Sobat River in the Sudan. He wrote of the kindness shown to him by the Sudanese natives—the Nuer, Nyuak, Dinka, and Shilluks. His adventures in the Sudan also became popular reading and undoubtedly stimulated the imagination of another generation. As he wrote on finding the Sobat source: "I mean that on one day we would see the course of the river, and on others, owing to the flatness of the country . . . we would lose sight of it . . . we were without it for some days."*

archaeologists. The Egyptian government funded the surveying and excavation of many important ancient sites before they were covered by water.

THE NEIGHBOR TO THE NORTH

Any study of Sudan must look closely at not only the River Nile, but at the strong influence of Egypt to the north, from ancient to modern times. The border area, the ancient kingdom of Nubia, is dry highlands, forming a natural barrier between the two countries. The peoples of Egypt and Sudan have communicated and traded for thousands of years, but geographic features have prevented large-scale intermingling and tribal relocation.

The geography here has fascinated, and intimidated, newcomers to the region for many centuries. Sir Samuel Baker, the British explorer of the 1860s, described his probe into the Nubian desert from Korosko in southern Egypt this way:

> We entered a dead level plain of orange-coloured sand, surrounded by pyramidical hills: the surface was strewn with objects resembling cannon shot and grape of all sizes. . . . [T]he spot looked like the old battle-field of some infernal region; rocks glowing with heat—not a vestige of vegetation—barren, withering desolation.— The slow rocking step of the camels was most irksome, and despite the heat, I dismounted to examine the Satanic bombs and cannon shot. Many of them were as perfectly round as though cast in a mould, others were egg-shaped, and all were hollow. With some difficulty I broke them, and found them to contain a bright red sand: they were, in fact, volcanic bombs that had been formed by the ejection of molten lava to a great height from active volcanoes; these had become globular in falling, and, having cooled before they reached the earth, they retained their forms as hard spherical bodies, precisely resembling cannon shot. . . .

> Passing through this wretched solitude we entered upon a scene of surpassing desolation. Far as the eye could reach were waves like a stormy sea, grey cool-looking waves in the burning heat; but no drop of water; it appeared as though a sudden curse had turned a raging sea to stone. . . .

This desolate land provided the Egyptians with an effective barrier between their civilization and the unpredictable warrior tribes of the African interior. At the same time, along the Nile and the camel routes, it was a neutral middle ground for traders.

During the last century and a half, Egypt's dependence on the River Nile has kept nervous eyes turned toward the south. "The Nile is life," Egyptians know. They have been leery of any development in Sudan that might affect the northerly flow of the river. For example, they feared that dams upstream, begun by the British, potentially could alter river levels downstream at times when irrigation would be affected. For that reason, the two countries control the Nile according to strict treaties that determine the storage level and release of impounded water. River levels are monitored closely from the Aswan Dam back to the headwaters of the White and Blue Niles. Scientists also record silt levels, rainfall, and rates of water evaporation.

THE RED SEA

The Red Sea is Sudan's other principal geographic feature. It is long and narrow, reaching to the north-northwest from the Indian Ocean. The Red Sea is 1,450 miles long and 225 miles across at its widest part. For a comparatively small body of salt-water, it reaches a surprising depth: almost 10,000 feet. It is particularly salty and very warm.

On the west, the Red Sea borders Egypt, Sudan, and Eritrea. Almost 500 miles of Sudanese shoreline is lapped by Red Sea waves. On the east is Saudi Arabia and Yemen.

Why is it called the Red Sea? Scholars suspect it is because of the red seaweed, *Rhodophyceae*, common to its waters. The Hebrew Bible refers to it as *yam suf*, the "sea of reeds." Others have speculated the sea got its name from red-hued coral; the Red Sea is noted for coral reefs along its shoreline. And from time to time, its waters are tinted after a heavy growth of algae dies off and turns reddish-brown.

In 1869 the Egyptians and French opened the Suez Canal, connecting the Mediterranean Sea to the northern end of the Red Sea. This meant ships could sail and steam between Europe and Asia without having to go around the huge African continent. The voyage of a cargo or passenger ship was shortened by a week or more. Naturally, the Red Sea thereafter became heavily traveled by deepwater vessels of many nations.

Before the canal was constructed, the Red Sea was an important nautical highway for traders and travelers between Africa and Asia. Across these waters, many Muslim sea merchants brought their goods and cultural influences from the Arabian Peninsula to the African mainland.

Major Cities

Sudan's largest urban area is its capital of Khartoum, along with the nearby municipalities of Omdurman and Khartoum North. (Omdurman, facing Khartoum across the White Nile, officially is the country's largest city.) Together, they have a population of more than one million. Khartoum lies in the fork of the White and Blue Nile rivers. The word "khartoum" refers to the shape of an elephant's trunk; the peninsula of land between the two merging rivers looks a bit like that.

Today, Khartoum is a city of modern buildings, a palace, churches and mosques, museums—even a zoo. Trees line the streets, giving it the effect of a desert oasis. An international airport here links Sudan to the world. Rail lines connect the capital to Egypt and Port Sudan . . . and indirectly to points beyond. Oil is piped directly from Khartoum to Port Sudan. And even today, as for centuries past, boats carry goods between Khartoum and river ports up and down the Nile and its tributaries.

In the mid-twentieth century, the airport at Khartoum became a busy hub for travelers between east and west Africa,

Ed-Dueim (Ad-Duwaym), 1919. *Ed-Dueim (Ad-Duwaym) is a city in the central Sudan on the western bank of the White Nile, about 87 miles southwest of Wad Madani, which has railroad and road connections with Khartoum. The city was a small Egyptian administrative post in the nineteenth century. Most of its inhabitants, mainly Arabic speaking, are related to northern Sudanese peoples. Today, Ed-Dueim is an agricultural center for the surrounding cotton-producing region. The latest area census dates to almost 30 years ago (1973). It listed some 26,000 people living in the city. This photograph was taken by Ernest Richmond, an intrepid British traveler who published a tourist guide to Cairo in 1908.*

and between the Mediterranean and the Cape of Good Hope at the continent's southern tip.

Modern Khartoum took shape as an army outpost in 1821. Because of its river fork location, it grew in military importance. This was obvious not only to outsiders who sought to control the region (the Egyptians and British) but to the natives. Khartoum was sacked during the Mahdist revolution of the 1880s. After the British-Egyptian army reclaimed Khartoum in 1898, they rebuilt the city and made it the seat of government. This status continued when Sudan declared its independence in 1956.

Khartoum today is the home of the Sudanese parliament, several universities, and the Sudan National Museum. It is a textile city, plus a center for manufacturing glass and gum.

Most people of Khartoum speak Arabic, but the city has much cultural diversity. This diversity results from the ongoing influx of people to this area from other parts of Africa.

Sudan's chief port is Port Sudan on the Red Sea. It has a population of about 200,000. Besides Khartoum and Port Sudan, the country's other large cities include Juba, the southern capital; El Obeid; and Wad Madani.

Arab Woman, Omdurman, 1899 *The coming of Islam changed Sudanese society. It facilitated the division of the country into north and south. Within a generation of the Prophet Muhammad's death in A.D. 632, Arab armies had carried Islam west from Arabia into North Africa. However, it took about 75 years for the Muslims to subjugate all of North Africa.*

The Arabs invaded Nubia—the northeastern Sudan— in A.D. 642 and again in A.D. 652. The Nubians put up a stout defense, causing the Arabs to accept an armistice. Subsequently, Arab commanders in Egypt concluded a series of regularly renewed treaties with the Nubians that governed relations between the two peoples for more than 600 years. So long as Arabs ruled Egypt, there was peace on the Nubian frontier.

Gradually through the centuries, the Nubian and Arab peoples seem to have merged. Although not all Muslims in the region are Arab-speaking, acceptance of Islam facilitated the Arabizing process. Forced conversion was rare. Rather, Islam penetrated the Sudan over a long period of time through intermarriage and contacts with Arab merchants and settlers. Exemption from taxation in regions under Muslim authority also proved a powerful incentive to conversion.

2

EARLY KINGDOMS

The first Sudanese were black-skinned hunter-gatherers. "Hunter-gatherer" is a term used by anthropologists. It refers to people all over the world, all through history, who have lived in small groups and wandered throughout certain regions. As the term suggests, they hunt wild animals and gather grain, roots, nuts, berries, and other items for their diets.

Stone-age tools have been found in different parts of Sudan. Archaeologists believe humans lived in sections of the Nile valley during the Paleolithic, or Old Stone Age, period—that is, for some thousands of years before the last ice age, which is thought to have occurred around 13,000 B.C. Different cultures, both African and Mediterranean, were settling along the Nile by 8000 B.C. and living in huts made of mud bricks. Ancient Sudanese made pottery and sandstone tools. By 3000 B.C., archaeologists believe, they were keeping cattle and other domesticated livestock.

ANCIENT NUBIA

Nubia was the ancient Nile valley kingdom in what is now northern Sudan and southern Egypt. It generally existed under the control of Egyptians or other foreigners throughout history who invaded and dominated Egypt and thus ruled Nubia. The

The Jabal River Rock Drawings *The earliest inhabitants of what is now the Sudan can be traced to peoples who lived in this area—the vicinity of Khartoum—during the Mesolithic period (Middle Stone Age: 30,000–20,000 B.C.). They were hunters and food gatherers who also made pottery from ground sandstone. Toward the end of the Neolithic Period (New Stone Age: 10,000–3000 B.C.), they had domesticated animals. Archaeological evidence convincingly tells us that these people were in contact with the predynastic Egyptian civilization to the north (before c. 2900 B.C.).*

kingdom was divided into two regions. In the north was Wawat. In the south was Kush (or Cush).

The Negroid people of Nubia are believed to have been fishers along the Red Sea and Nile, hunters elsewhere. By about 3000 B.C., farming had become a way of life for many area inhabitants. They brought their basic crops from both the west (modern-day Chad and Libya) and north (Egypt). Eight hundred years later, northern Nubia apparently was infiltrated by a race of Caucasian herders. Sheep, cows, and goats began grazing in the Nile valley.

For much of its history, Nubia was ruled by viceroys appointed by the Egyptian pharaoh. Deputies of the viceroy ruled Wawat and Kush individually. Although Egyptians were the chief officials, most of the daily administration of government and justice was carried out by native Nubians. These local administrators became an elite class of natives. Some of them and their families adopted the Egyptian language.

This has been the way shrewd occupying forces have "governed" their conquered lands for centuries, in different scenarios around the world. The Europeans who claimed control of Africa in the late 1800s, for example, were far too few in number to control every action of the people. Moreover, they cared little how the natives went about their lives—as long as the rulers could control trade in the region and persuade or force the locals to pay them taxes. By letting friendly natives make the everyday decisions to solve ordinary problems, Europeans found it fairly easy to "rule" and prosper in Africa.

KUSH CONQUERS EGYPT

Of Nubia's two regions, Kush became an especially important kingdom for several reasons: location, geographic features, and natural riches. Trade routes from Red Sea ports fanned out across Kush into southern Egypt and the Sahara, and southwestward toward the center of Africa. Farming peoples were attracted to the fertile soil around the River Nile.

H. W. Seton-Karr, Northern Sudan, 1899 *H. W. Seton-Karr reported for* The Times *(London), one of Great Britain's oldest and most influential newspapers, on the Battle of Omdurman (1899). Karr also was an archaeologist who specialized in prehistoric tools, which he dug for in Egypt. In 1901 the Italian government honored him with the Galileo Medal.*

Seton-Karr wired many stories about Egypt and the Sudan to The Times. *Perhaps his most noted one was his description of the discovery of an ancient Egyptian emerald mine in 1897–98. Before Egyptian mining laws, he wrote how many emeralds were "forwarded to me by the civil governor" as a gift. Karr donated these emeralds to the British Museum. He gave his extensive anthropological photographic collection to the Royal Geographical Society in 1909.*

Gold and emeralds were found in the Kush highlands, providing Egyptian kings with part of their fabled wealth. The Egyptians also carried home useful animal hides, ivory tusks, and incense. They forced Nubian slaves not only to perform backbreaking labor, but to serve as soldiers. The Egyptians built forts farther and farther south along the Nile and sent military expeditions regularly into the desert. Slave-soldiers from Kush found themselves helping capture some of their own kindred!

Egyptian influences were felt as far south as present-day Khartoum, where the White and Blue Nile rivers merge.

Egypt was invaded about 1720 B.C. by the Hyksos, powerful Arabian nomads. During their reign, Kush became largely isolated from its Egyptian overlords and was left to develop on its own. Although the Hyksos gradually were driven out of Egypt, by 1000 B.C. Egypt was on the decline as a North African power, but Kush had become quite strong. Under King Piankhi in the eighth century B.C., the Kushites actually took control of Egypt, reversing the tradition of dominance between the two lands.

When you think of the great pyramids, you think of Egypt. Northern Sudan also has pyramids, however. From the Egyptians, the rulers of Kush took the idea of burying their sovereigns within these giant constructions. The largest pyramid in Sudan, the burial place of the seventh-century King Taharqa, is found in Nuri.

Kush remained a strong kingdom for another thousand years. Whereas Egypt absorbed the cultural influences of the ancient Persians, Greeks, and Romans who successively overran it, Kush held on to its predominant African influences. It developed its own language and worshiped its own gods, in addition to Amon Re and other Egyptian gods.

In the early fourth century A.D., armies from the kingdom of Aksum in what is now Ethiopia conquered the Kushite capital at Meroe and the towns along the Nile. The kingdom of Kush effectively was ended.

The Jabal River Rock Drawings *One main tributary of the Nile River, flowing south to north, enters the Sudan at Nimule and from there to Juba—a distance of some 120 miles—it is called the Al-Jabal River or Mountain Nile. This section of the river descends through narrow gorges; it is not commercially navigable. Below Juba, the river flows over a long and very level clay plain. It is along this route of the river—from Nimule to Juba—that early twentieth century archaeologists discovered primitive rock drawings dating back to pre-historic times.*

CHRISTIANS AND ARABS

Little is known of the history of northern Sudan from the fall of Kush until the Christian missionaries Julian and Longinus arrived during the sixth century A.D. Christianity began to thrive along the Nile in Nubia, as well as in the Beja region of the Red Sea. The missionaries built not only churches, but schools. They encouraged education and cultural refinement.

The following century, though, Egypt and Nubia were overrun by Arab invaders from across the Red Sea. A powerful Arab army pressed up the Nile from Egypt, destroying Christian churches and cathedrals. They laid siege to the cities, using catapults to hurl huge stones against the buildings. These invaders were Muslims, followers of the prophet Muhammad. With religious zeal, they were expanding all across northern Africa—and in other directions from their Arabian homelands.

They were not strong enough to occupy Nubia, however. The Arabs forged a treaty with the native kingdoms. They agreed no Arabs would settle in Nubia, and no Nubians would cross the dry plains to settle in Egypt. The Arabs would provide Nubia with annual gifts of grain and horses; Nubia would provide the Arabs with slaves and gems. For the next 600 years, Nubia and Egypt carried on peaceful trade.

For the Nubians, the treaty quieted fears of invasion from the north. For the Arabs who ruled Egypt, it provided a secure "frontier" in the south, a friendly buffer between Egypt and interior African kingdoms. Although tribes of Arab nomads sometimes raided into the northern Nubian desert seeking gold, there was no organized attempt at invasion.

It was at this point in history that what eventually would become the Republic of the Sudan began to take the form of a land divided, north and south. Already the cultural differences were striking—ancient African in the south, Arabian in the north. Increasingly, political and social distinctions would become more marked as well.

SLAVES TAKE COMMAND: THE MAMLUKS

This period of relative peace ended in the late 1200s after Egypt was taken over by the Mamluks. Mamluks were slaves who were used as soldiers by the Arabian caliphs who ruled Egypt. The slaves were very effective and valuable warriors. They also were cunning. In 1250 Mamluk soldiers gained control of the Eyptian palace. Mamluk sultans reigned for the next two and a half centuries.

The Mamluks began to send armies into Nubia, hoping to expand their control to the south. By the 1500s these raids had become ventures not of greed but of necessity: Ottoman Turks were overrunning Egypt. The Mamluks were being pushed out by a new group of invaders!

Although they failed to subdue the Nubian kingdom altogether, the Mamluk attacks left it pillaged and weak. Ignoring the long-standing treaty, Arab tribes began to settle in the area and brought their livestock to graze along the middle Nile. Over the ensuing generations, Arabs and Nubians intermarried; in time, through these marriages, the Arabs gained the upper hand. Meanwhile, the Muslim culture mingled with the Nubians' Christianity.

The southern Nubian kingdom, Alwah, remained a predominantly Christian society throughout most of this period of upheaval. Scholars believe, however, that it probably had developed a unique form of Christian worship by the 1400s because it had little communication with mainline Christianity. Gradually, Arab raids during the 1400s chipped away at Alwah's resources and defense. It fell to the Arabs at the end of the century.

THE FUNJ DYNASTY

Soon, the new Arab settlers in Nubia came under attack themselves. The threat now was from the fierce Funj (also spelled Fung) people who lived to the southeast along the Blue Nile. This is today the border area between Sudan and Ethiopia.

The Funj had established a capital at Sennar, about 200 miles up the Blue Nile from its confluence with the White Nile. Sennar's location made it an excellent trading center. Through it passed ivory, ebony, coffee, animal hides and exotic feathers, gum, minerals, and—unhappily—slaves from the African interior. From Nubia and Egypt in the north came cloth, tools, and jewelry.

Many tribes paid homage to the Funj leader, called the "mek," in return for protection and for keeping law and order. Local tribes were ruled by chiefs, "head men," or minor "kings." Some tribes ritually killed their chiefs when they no longer considered them to be strong leaders. When that happened, tribal rule did not necessarily descend to the oldest son or daughter as in some cultures. It might pass, for example, to a cousin or to the son of a previous head man.

Predictably, many tribal chiefs lived in constant fear of their lives, as did some of their prospective successors, who continually suspected deadly plots by rivals. Those rivals, in many instances, were blood relatives!

While the Arabs were spreading further southward from Egypt in the early 1500s, the Funj were reaching northward for new territory to settle. Inevitably, the two cultures fought. In the decisive battle near Arbaji on the Blue Nile, the Funj won a great victory. For the next three centuries, they controlled the region.

Although victorious, the Funj were influenced heavily by the Arabs. As early as the mid-1500s, many of the Funj, including some of their rulers, were becoming Muslims, at least in principle. Muslim holy men played important leadership roles in daily life (and still do today). They established Muslim schools, and their followers obtained dominant government roles. Neverless, the Funj retained many distinctly African customs as well.

Funj kings gradually widened their domain, pushing westward toward the Sahara Desert during the seventeenth and eighteenth centuries. They also battled with the Ethiopians to the

Sultan Idris, Darfunj, c. 1922 *Sultan Idris claimed to be a direct descendent of the Funj kings. The Funj dynasty ruled the Darfunj area of the Sudan between the sixteenth and eighteenth centuries. This area is south of Khartoum, between the Blue Nile and the White Nile rivers.*

The Funj state, a confederation of Nilotic tribes, under the rule of a sultan, stood between the Arabs in the north, the Ethiopians in the east, and the non-Muslim blacks in the south. The Funj capital, Sennar, was located on the Blue Nile, south of Khartoum. During the last half of the eighteenth century, the Funj kingdom disintegrated because of internal intrigues and wars with Ethiopians. In 1821 Egyptian soldiers captured Sennar, and the Funj empire passed into oblivion.

east. Usually victorious, they seemed unstoppable. However, disaster eventually rocked the dynasty from within. The Funj army, made up of slaves, became very powerful, not just in battle but as a growing aristocratic class in the capital of Sennar. The army overthrew King Unsa III in 1718. For the next century power was held successively by royal Funj kings and military leaders. The once great dynasty weakened and was ill-prepared to fend off a coming invasion from the north.

Nuba Village, 1904 *The cylindrical hut with white facing (upper center-right of photograph) is a Nuba village storehouse. Here, they keep their precious grain. Nuba huts, made of mud which dries to concrete-like hardness, are thatched with pointed or conical roofs. A tribesman's entire household possessions comprise a few gourds, some baskets and pots, and a plank bed. Wives and children usually live in one hut, the husband in another.*

3

THE EUROPEANS
ARRIVE

As Funj authority declined, Egyptian invaders reappeared in the north of Sudan. By the 1820s Egypt had defeated the last of the old kingdoms and effectively ruled the country. The Egyptian sultans began to rely heavily on European support to maintain their authority. England and France had jockeyed for influence in the area since the 1700s. In 1798–99, Napoleon Bonaparte led a French army in an outright invasion of Egypt. Great Britain joined the Turks and repelled Napoleon's forces.

The Turks remained in power, but this war left Egypt in disarray. The Turks needed desperately to stabilize their Nile domain. To do so, they appointed a domineering new governor, or "pasha," in 1805: Muhammad Ali. One of Ali's first actions as the Turks' viceroy of Egypt was to drive from the country the remaining Mamluks, whom he feared would challenge his authority. This he did with an Ottoman army consisting of soldiers from southern Europe.

Ali ultimately turned his attention to the south. The Egyptian-controlled governor in Sudan was complaining of the Mamluks. After their retreat from Egypt, some of the Mamluks had set up an independent slave-trading base at Dunqulah. They operated in defiance of the Sudanese administration.

In 1821, Muhammad Ali dispatched his son Ibrahim Pasha to invade the region and set up an Egyptian government at Khartoum. This administration became known as the Turkiyah (Turkish) government in Sudan.

THE SLAVE TRADE

Above all, Ali wanted to control the slave trade along the White Nile. Slaves were vital to the Egyptian army. For the next half century, expeditions probed between the Blue and White Nile rivers southeast of Khartoum, capturing natives and sending them north. Some historians believe the most intense slave trading in the region's history occurred during Ali's reign. One tribe, the Bongo people, is estimated to have dwindled from a population of about 100,000 to 5,000 because of the slavers.

Slave trading had been a leading form of "commerce" in the area for centuries. Slave holding was protected by law and treaty. In the great treaty between the invading Muslims and Christian inhabitants of Nubia about A.D. 640, one stipulation of the Arabs read: "Ye shall give us the slaves of Muslims who seek refuge among you, and send them back to the country of Islam." Another: "Every year ye shall pay 360 head of slaves to the leader of the Muslims, of the middle class of slaves of your country, without bodily defects, males and females, but no old men nor old women nor young children." Finally: "If ye harbour a Muslim slave . . . or withhold any of the 360 head of slaves, then this promised peace and security will be withdrawn from you, and we shall revert to hostility. . . ."

By 1837 reports of the brutality of the slave trade sent shock waves through Europe. In that year, a traveler named Ignatius Pallme from Bohemia (in modern-day Czechoslovakia) witnessed slave raids and recorded what he saw. The Turkish merchants were particularly merciless. Slavers of previous eras had sought able-bodied men and women; now they were taking old, feeble natives and even children. Some of their victims committed suicide rather than let themselves be taken captive. Those

taken alive were beaten with musket stocks, poked with bayo-
nets, and whipped savagely.

To prevent adult prisoners from escaping during the long
march to market, which might take weeks, the captors tied
lengths of tree trunks awkwardly to their necks. Youngsters had
their hands tied together in groups. These bindings rubbed the
skin raw; the wounds went untreated, resulting in infection and
in some cases permanent disability. Stragglers were flogged. If
they could not walk, they were dragged through the sand by
camels. At the beginning of the next day's march, prisoners who
had become too weak to continue were left behind to die, without food or water.

At the slave-trading center of Lobeid, the strongest of the captured men were pressed into military service. Other slaves were
sold to the highest bidder at the auction block—or were turned
over as payment to soldiers who once had been slaves themselves. These soldiers typically had been waiting for many
months for some form of wages. Wanting cash, the soldiers usually sold their "pay" slaves, in turn, at market. Wrote Pallme:

> It is not an uncommon occurrence for a son to find his
> own father, or a father his son, assigned to him, or for a
> brother to become the possessor of his brother; but he is
> forced in defiance of the feelings of nature to sell him,
> in order to share the proceeds with a comrade who is co-
> proprietor of the slave with him. Officers and privates
> are obliged to receive these slaves at a certain valuation
> in lieu of money, and generally sell them at a loss. . . .
>
> No pen can describe the cruelties these miserable men
> were made to suffer, in addition to the mental torment
> consequent on their loss of freedom; for laden with the
> heavy sheba [tree trunk] round their necks, or bound
> together with tight straps or handcuffs, the poor Negroes
> were driven on like cattle, but treated with far less care
> or forebearance. The greater number of them, covered
> with the wounds they had received in battle, or excori-
> ated by the sheba, or the straps, and handcuffs, were put

to yet severer trials on the road, and, if too exhausted to keep pace with the transport, the most cruel punishment awaited them; the piercing cry of complaint of these unfortunate beings, and the tears and sobs of the children who had either lost their parents in the capture of the village, or were too tired to follow their exhausted mothers, would have melted a heart of stone to pity. . . .

The shrieks and sobs of the children, the cries of the wounded, and the groans of the sick, were perfectly horrifying. . . . I am unequal to the task of narrating all the horrors I witnessed during the few days I attached myself to the convoy. . . .

Many slaves arrived at market barely able to move but still alive. That was very important to the captors. They cared not whether their prisoners were alive or dead the following day, as long as they were alive when they were tallied at market. Pallme explained that "the sole object is to furnish the number of slaves demanded by the government."

The most extraordinary part of that distressing comment was the last: "demanded by the government." With an Egyptian regime that not only condoned but *depended* on slavery, the natives of Sudan were doomed to hellish, unmitigated raids for several generations. Thousands of slaves were taken from southern Sudan every year. Until 1843 the slave raids all were conducted by the government. After that, Ali's administration continued its official slave trade but also licensed private merchants to participate—for a fee.

THE QUEST FOR IVORY

After Great Britain began exerting greater influence in the region, the Egyptian viceroys came under pressure to end the Sudanese slave trade. There was little they could do for many years, however. Muhammad Ali had ended slave-trading monopolies, but slave trading continued briskly. The British succeeded in decreasing the transportation of African slaves into Asian countries, but slave trading continued within Africa itself. In 1860, after Ali's death, Egypt abolished slavery by law—yet still the practice continued.

During the mid-1800s, the quest for ivory became as intense as slave trading. According to historians Roland Oliver and J.D. Fage, "It was the search for ivory, rather than that for slaves, which took the coastmen annually further and further into the interior [by the 1870s]. . . ." But, they pointed out, ivory trading did not replace slave trading. In fact, slave labor was necessary to support large-scale elephant hunts, carrying the hunting expeditions' supplies and bringing the unwieldy ivory tusks out of the interior to the trading ports. Slaves used in the ivory trade, wrote Oliver and Fage, "might never cross the wide seas to an external market, but they were nevertheless removed by violence from their homes and ultimately sold."

Some historians believe Muhammad Ali's sons, who ruled as khedives (or viceroys) after him, personally opposed slave trading but saw no way to stop it. The ivory trade had become important in the region's economy, and slave labor was needed to operate the ivory trade at a profit.

Throughout the life of Muhammad Ali, his rule did not go unchallenged. He taxed the people oppressively, extracting not just money but livestock—as well as slaves. His soldiers treated the natives cruelly, demanded tribute, and sacked some of the ancient pyramids in search of riches. Rebellious natives killed Ali's son, burning him alive. The Turkish regime in Egypt retaliated furiously.

Sudan floundered dismally during the mid-1800s. A succession of short-term governors-general accomplished little. At one point, the Egyptian viceroy became so frustrated he temporarily did away with the governors-general and gave orders directly to the lesser leaders in Sudan.

UNEASY NEWCOMERS IN AN ALIEN LAND

Most European explorers, merchants, adventurers, and missionaries in the nineteenth century who sought to carve footholds in the Sudan landscape didn't see the country as an attractive place to live. Rather, they saw it as an important geographic crossroads in what has been called the Europeans' "scramble for Africa." With scattered exceptions, Sudan was to them a desolate place that presented hardships, uncertainties, and no few hazards.

Alessandro Dal Bosco was a 28-year-old Italian missionary in Khartoum in 1858. To him, Khartoum was "ugly and unsightly . . . , consisting only of hovels and mud huts." He described roads "full of potholes" and a maze of mysterious alleys "like a labyrinth." "The roads, in fact, are not like those of Europe, passing through the town from one side to the other, but almost all of them lead to this or that house, which is enclosed by a wall, making it impossible to find a way round."

Dal Bosco wrote that the low, mud-brick houses were so badly built that during the rainy season they tended to collapse into the street. "[I]f the rain falls with its usual intensity during the night, the occupant of some such miserable house sits with trembling heart fearing to see his hovel reduced to a heap of mud at any moment. He will also have to think of finding refuge from the water which is coming through a hole in the roof and, by flooding the house, forcing him to abandon it."

Luigi Montuori, another missionary writing from the same region a few years earlier, chronicled the perils of travel between villages. His party moved only during the brightest part of the afternoon because of the danger of lions.

> After we had been on our way for about half-an-hour we began to hear frightening roars coming from several directions, not more than 40 or 50 feet away. Bones and skulls lay everywhere, while sandals and clothes had been torn to shreds and then scattered in all directions by the wind. This appalling sight frightened not only the members of our caravan but also the camels and mules. In particular, my mule was so frightened that it no longer heeded the bridle, and bucked violently until I was thrown heavily to the ground, severely injuring my face. I lay there stunned

Nuba Village, 1904 *The Nuba rank among the most primitive tribes of the Sudan. Their main crops are millet, corn, and peanuts. They also keep cattle, sheep, and goats. Nuba religious practices are linked with agricultural rituals; annual sacrifices are made to ancestral spirits; and priestly experts and rain-makers hold an important position in their society.*

The Nuba prepare delicious dishes from millet and corn. This staple menu is varied with live honey-covered flies and locusts. They also eat snakes, monkey, dogs, and all sorts of birds.

for some time suffering greatly from the wounds. Then
I was bandaged as well as possible under the circum-
stances; the blood that covered me was wiped away,
I was helped onto my mule and the journey
continued. . . .

River travel had risks, as well. Along certain parts of the
Nile, boatmen would not travel at night because of frequent

Sesame Press, Omdurman, 1919 *The Sudan is one of the poorest and least developed countries in the world. Most of its inhabitants depend upon farming and animal husbandry for their meager livelihood. Sesame, cotton, and peanuts are the Sudan's chief crops. Since antiquity, sesame has been cultivated for its seeds, which are used as food and flavoring—and from which its prized oil is extracted. Sesame oil is used as a salad or cooking oil and in the manufacture of soaps, cosmetics, and pharmaceuticals. It is also used as a lubricant.*

This is a photograph of a primitive sesame press. The power is provided by a dromedary. A modern press exerts pressures as high as 30,000 pounds per square inch!

shifts in the channels and shoals. Crocodiles intimidated Europeans who ventured up the Nile from Egypt in small vessels or along the riverbank trails. Huge flies, especially in the southern swamps, posed not only annoyances but health hazards. And the Nile is home to as many as 15 species of poisonous snakes!

At the same time, the newcomers had to marvel at the seasonal changes that quickly could spread breathtaking beauty across desolate terrain. A third Italian correspondent from the mid-nineteenth century, Giovanni Beltrame, wrote of the transformation he witnessed along the Blue Nile near Sennar:

> For six or seven months of the year, Sinnar presents a grim picture of barrenness but, as soon as the rainy season starts [in May], the scene changes entirely: one or two heavy rains are sufficient to produce a complete change with the ground covered with vegetation. The soil is fertile. The inhabitants of Sinnar cultivate only a very small portion of their land: the harvest is sufficient to provide the country for at least three years. The principal products are: durra, wheat, maize, beans, lentils and tobacco. In the plains, watered by the Dindir [a tributary river flowing into the Blue Nile between Sennar and Khartoum], the finest quality cotton and sesame are easily grown. The gardens, irrigated daily by the water from the river, produce pomegranates, oranges, lemons and figs either in flower or fruit practically all the year round. . . .

But many foreigners continued to find the Sudan climate intolerable at certain times of year, for generations to come. Writing around 1950, commentator Mekki Abbas reported:

> The cool dry winter of Khartoum attracts European and American tourists and visitors, but its dry heat in the summer, which reaches an average maximum of 109° in the shade, drives almost all the British officials away to England and brings the main activities of the government, and with them the political life of the country, almost to a standstill.

Shilluks, 1899 *The Shilluks are a Nilotic people along the west bank of the Bahr-al-Jabal section of the Nile River in the southern Sudan. With access to fairly good land along the Nile, they rely heavily on farming and fishing for subsistence. Cattle holdings are considered a sign of wealth.*

The Shilluks have permanent settlements and do not move regularly in search of food. Traditionally, their ruler is both a political and religious one—and each king, reth, at the time of his investiture becomes the reincarnation of the mystical Nyikang, the first Shilluk. Anthropologists differ about the power of the reth but most agree that his health is closely related to the material and spiritual welfare of the Shilluks. It is likely that the unity of the Shilluk people, under a divine-right ruler and the permanence of their settlements, contributed to a stable social structure. This centralization enabled the Shilluks to preserve their tribal integrity in face of the external political pressures of the nineteenth and twentieth centuries.

4

THE FAR REACH OF
GREAT BRITAIN

Into the last half of the nineteenth century, much of what is now Sudan was ruled by the "Khartoum Arabs," or Turks. These were the succession of khedives appointed by the Turkish sultan to govern Egypt and Sudan. Inevitably, this led to a powerful European influence. With the appointment of Ismail Pasha as viceroy in 1863, European-style leadership came to bear on Sudan.

Ismail had studied in Austria and France, as well as Egypt. He dreamed of bringing Egypt and Sudan into the "modern" world—that is, to develop northeastern Africa using Western ideas and inventions. In his vision for a prosperous, expanding Egypt, Ismail was keenly interested in such projects as the Suez Canal. He also looked far southward from Cairo, the Egyptian capital. Ismail hoped to control not just Sudan but the entire upper Nile, all the way to the interior African lakes near the river's head-waters.

Four years after he was appointed viceroy of Egypt, Ismail was named khedive, a hereditary title, by the Turkish sultan. Ismail sought financial support for his plans from European investors. They were interested, but they were displeased by the continuing slave trade in the region. Would Ismail make a serious effort to stop slave trading in Sudan once and for all? Yes, he pledged. Thus, Egyptian expansion up the

Nile—backed by European money and power—began in earnest.

We learned at the beginning of the book how Samuel White Baker, an Englishman, in the early 1860s explored the region of what came to be called the Albert Nile more than 100 miles south of Sudan. Searching for the sources of the great Nile, Baker discovered a sizeable lake, which he named Albert Nyanza, or Lake Albert. This lake is located between the modern-day countries of Zaire and Uganda.

Ismail Pasha in 1869 asked Baker to lead another expedition into the interior. Baker was to explore the upper Nile more fully, annex the territory for Egypt, and quash the slave trade. Baker succeeded, for the most part. For his reward, he was made governor-general of this new province, called Equatoria because of its proximity to the equator. Baker was not a popular administrator, however. He offended Ismail's Muslim government officials and was disliked by some of the native tribes. As Ismail quickly discovered, Baker had achieved only a partial victory over the slave traders. Baker had struck down the slave stations of the upper Nile but had done nothing to stop slave taking in the plains to the west. And it was there that a serious threat was growing to challenge Ismail's scheme of expansion.

The most powerful slave merchant was Zubayr Pasha. Eventually, he took over all the slave trade in the Bahr Al-Ghazal plains. Using firearms against the natives' spears, his men easily captured thousands of people in the interior and marched them to slave trading posts in Egypt.

The Egyptian government could not mount a force strong enough to stop Zubayr's operations. Instead, in order to establish control over his operations (or, at least, the *appearance* of control), they made Zubayr the governor-general of the plains! Zubayr's slave traders continued their tragic work, now as government administrators.

While Ismail Pasha's influence was slipping away in this ignoble manner in the south, an internationally celebrated achievement in the northeast was occurring that would have a much more decisive effect in the Egypt/Sudan power game. For many centuries, regional civilizations had sought to connect the Red Sea by water with the Nile delta and, in effect, with the Mediterranean Sea. In 1854 the reigning Egyptian khedive granted rights for building a canal to a Frenchman named Ferdinand de Lesseps. Work on the narrow, 100-mile-long waterway through the Isthmus of Suez in northeastern Egypt began in 1859. It took 10 years to complete.

Although it was primarily a French construction project, the Suez Canal was of keen interest to all the European powers. In 1875 British Prime Minister Benjamin Disraeli managed to acquire from Ismail Pasha a controlling interest in the canal for England. Great Britain now had, in the world's eyes, an undeniable excuse to bring military force to bear in the region. No one could downplay the importance of the new canal. Through Disraeli's skillful bargaining, England had obtained a strong measure of international rights in protecting the passageway. Within a few years, Great Britain would become the dominant force in the whole Suez realm.

Baker retired in 1873 as governor-general of Equatoria. Ismail Pasha replaced him with Charles George Gordon, a celebrated British army commander. Gordon established a semblance of Egyptian authority in the region, breaking up Zubayr's massive slavery operation. But many of the native peoples remained basically independent, oblivious to this "Europeanization" of Africa that was going on around them.

In 1877 Gordon was made governor-general of all Sudan. Ismail Pasha that year formally agreed with the British to push for an end to slave trading in Sudan. Gordon carried out this assignment, raiding slave stations throughout Sudan and jailing the traders. Some of the slave merchants were hanged.

In time, Gordon became even less liked among the natives than Baker. The slave trade, though horribly inhumane, had become an important fixture in the area's economy. Gordon's crackdown on slaving brought hard times. Muslim natives resented this Christian Englishman's policies. He soon resigned.

Hamid Bey Fatin, Nazir of the Hamar Degagin Region, 1905 *In the 1870s Hamid was appointed a bey—a regional governor—in the Sudan by General Charles Gordon. Gordon, a British general, had become a national hero for his bravery during the Crimean War (1853–56) and his exploits in China (1860–65). In 1873 the khedive of Egypt—the governing viceroy of the Sultan of Turkey—appointed Gordon governor of the southern Sudanese province of Equatoria. (Egypt and the Sudan were then part of the Ottoman Empire.) The khedive regularly hired Europeans for his administrative staff. Gordon's instructions were to extend Turkish rule to the heart of central Africa in order to crush the slave trade.*

Gordon established his personal authority over a vast area of the southern Sudan—mapping the upper Nile River, crushing rebellions, and suppressing the slave trade. In 1880 ill health forced him to resign his position and return to England.

While tension increased in Sudan, Ismail's administration in Egypt fell apart. He had placed Egypt into heavy debt to European powers. These debts could not be paid. At last, European creditors forced the Turkish sultan to remove Ismail from office in 1879. The Europeans took over Egypt's financial administration themselves.

This situation left Egypt, and especially Sudan, very unstable. The country officially was under Egyptian authority, but the Egyptian government was in such disarray that it could not oversee the southern territory effectively. Egypt was in no condition to resist when, in 1881, a native leader propelled himself to popularity. His name was Muhammad Ahmad ibn Abd Allah. To his followers, he became known as the Mahdi—the "divinely guided one."

The Ruins of El Obeid (Al Ubayyi), 1900 *Politics in the modern Sudan begins with al-Mahdi (1844–85). Between 1881 and 1885, al-Mahdi (Arabic: "Guided One") triumphantly threw off Turco-Egyptian-British Control. In those four years, al-Mahdi created a vast Islamic state extending from the Red Sea to Central Africa. The Mahdi, a messianic holy man, was both a spiritual and a political ruler. More than a century later, the movement that he founded is still influential in the Sudan.*

In 1880, the Sudan was a dependency of Egypt, which was itself a province of the Ottoman Empire. In appearance, education, and general way of life, the Turkish rulers of the Sudan sharply contrasted with their subjects. Al-Mahdi, who combined a personal magnetism with religious zealotry, appealed to the discontented and oppressed Sudanese. In 1881 he proclaimed his divine mission to both restore Islam in the Sudan to its primitive purity and to replace the government which had defiled it. Within four years, by 1885, al-Mahdi had established a theocratic state in the Sudan with its capital at Omdurman. Early in 1882 al-Mahdi proclaimed a jihad, or holy war, against Turkish authority. He and his adherents made a long march into the Kordofan, the central Sudan, to gain recruits. The following year (November 5, 1883), al-Mahdi's supporters, armed with spears and swords, annihilated an 8,000-man Egyptian force commanded by British General William Hicks near El Obeid (al-Ubayyi). They seized the Egyptian rifles and ammunition. Now 30,000-strong, the Mahdi followers followed up their victory by laying siege to El Obeid and starved it into submission after four months.

5

THE MAHDIST REVOLT

The Mahdi rose to power almost overnight—or so it seemed to the far-removed European public. One year the British and Egyptians were administering a fragile but seemingly stable Sudan state. The next the Mahdi's armies were everywhere, overrunning outposts and towns, uprooting the established order. What was happening? And who was the Mahdi?

To understand his dramatic rise to popularity, we need to consider briefly the existing ideals and authorities the Mahdi so vehemently opposed. Foremost were the Egyptian government officials, manipulated by the Ottoman Turks, who administrated Sudan affairs. In the eyes of the Mahdi and many of the Sudanese population, the Ottomans had three strikes against them: (1) they were foreigners, different from Sudan's natives in their customs, language, and even in the way they looked; (2) they practiced a brand of Islam the Mahdists considered impure; and (3) they were making a royal mess of government in Egypt and Sudan.

Meanwhile, here had come the British—foreigners from even further away than the Turks. Their expedition leaders had interfered with Sudan's profitable slave trade and, ironically, infuriated many of the natives. The English clearly did not understand the Sudanese and their way of life. Great Britain, like other European countries of the period, arrived to lay claim to strategic sections of Africa. The Europeans hoped to extend their own power by establishing trading privileges and other forms of control on the mysterious continent. Near the top of England's wish list in the "scramble for Africa" was the Nile, an ambition that was not lost on shrewd native leaders.

Sudan at first was not a specific part of the Europeans' pompous "partitioning" of the continent. Soon, though, it attracted the attention of the British and French, who had been trading in the region for many years. Sudan was important to them because, as we've seen, it is the land of the middle Nile. The European country that controlled trade along the Nile obviously would control most of the trade into and out of northeastern Africa. Sudan also was important as a general connecting region between the Arab north/northeast and the largely unexplored interior of Africa where the Europeans expected to find a variety of riches.

For the moment, the Europeans were in no position to exert very much control over Sudan. The unexpected phenomenon of the Mahdi complicated things. Soon raging Mahdist armies would not only block British designs but oust the British leadership that, in league with the Egyptians, had entrenched itself in Sudan.

A Passion for Islam

The Mahdi came to power in Sudan during the early 1880s. Born in the Nubian city of Dongola (Dunqulah) in 1844, he was the son of a boat builder. His family were devout followers of Islam. His father was said to be a descendant of Muhammad, the Islamic prophet himself.

Muhammad Ahmad became absorbed in Islam at an early age. He probably could have obtained a formal Islamic education in Cairo and become part of the professional religious leadership, perhaps as a Muslim judge. That was not for him, however. He came to despise the Ottoman form of Islamic practice and rule. He believed the Turks, over the centuries, had strayed from the original teachings of the prophet Muhammad.

So he stayed in his home country where, removed from the reigning religious order, he could immerse himself in what he felt were the true precepts of Islam.

For awhile Muhammad Ahmad studied the traditions of the Sufi, a mystic Muslim order. As a young man, he joined the Muslim order called the Sammaniyah. In time, he became critical even of his teacher, or "shaykh." He set himself apart, convinced of his destiny to bring about a Muslim revival, and he began to attract a small following. With some of these devotees, he took to the island of Aba in the middle of the White Nile. There, in seclusion, he lived a life of austerity, disciplining himself in deep study of the Muslim faith. What the people needed, he insisted, was a return to the pure form of Muslim that was practiced in Muhammad's time, 12 centuries earlier. He and his followers advocated a lifestyle of self-denial, refusing to indulge in liquor or smoking. Women were restricted to lives of subservience in the home.

In 1880 Muhammad Ahmad left his river island and traveled through the Kordofan (Kurufan) region of Sudan. The restlessness of the people was obvious. They resented the Egyptian-English government administration. They were taxed ruthlessly, and if they couldn't pay or did not pay on time, they were whipped. Poor natives were expected to perform menial and backbreaking tasks for the governing class. Times were very hard.

The Mahdi was supported by Sudan's faqihs, or holy men, who despised the Egyptian occupiers and their altered brand of Islam. Under Turkish control, a form of "orthodox" Islam (which encouraged cooperation with the Ottoman rulers) had been promoted. This was not true Islam, many Sudanese people and holy men claimed. These traditionalists were eager to follow a new leader who would return them to the original Muslim faith.

Sinister elements of Sudanese society inflamed the dangerous mood. The old slave traders were incensed because their grotesque work was being disrupted by the likes of Baker and Gordon. Aggressive tribal chiefs were infuriated when their own raids of invasion or retaliation against other tribes were interrupted by government forces. Fragmented, the slave merchants and local chiefs were not powerful enough to challenge the ruling authority. But if a charismatic native visionary could mass popular support, perhaps this leader could throw off the offending Ottoman administration. Such a guide would be worth following. Perhaps Muhammad Ahmad was the very leader they hoped for. If they supported him and helped him drive out the khedive leadership, then their own former power and wealth might be restored.

MOMENTUM!

Muhammad Ahmad's following grew larger and larger. In June 1881 he proclaimed himself the "Mahdi," the Muslim Messiah. The Mahdi offered the people hope and vowed to vanquish the infidel government—but he required complete sovereignty. He demanded that the people of the region join his movement or be prepared to be destroyed by it. To him, there was no middle ground.

To the native people, it seemed time for the Mahdi's arrival. The Muslim calendar had reached the end of a century. A new century should bring an end to their economic and political darkness and restore light, as well, to their traditional faith. How was Muhammad Ahmad to wrest power from the Egyptian regime, though? He needed more than a circle of faqihs to effect a takeover. The supportive slave merchants, while certainly brutal enough, were no army.

He found the heart of his army in the form of the Baqqarah Arabs, a nomadic people who herded cattle in the regions of Kordofan and Darfur west of the Nile. With them at the forefront, the followers of the Mahdi—"Dervishes" the Europeans called them—took control of their homeland in 1882 and 1883. Some government strongholds they overran; others they besieged and starved until the foes surrendered. They captured British rifles and even artillery pieces as well as gold and other valuables. They strengthened from a small, primitively armed force to a massive, formidably equipped army zealously bent on a mission.

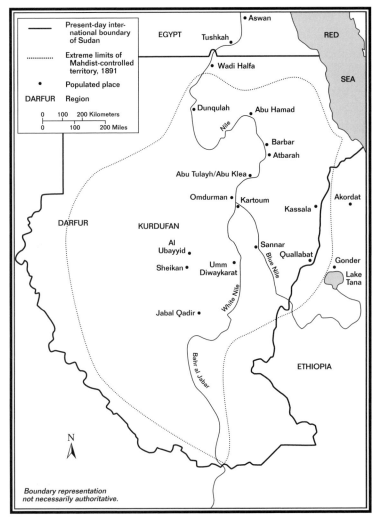

The Mahdist State, 1881–98.

In early November 1883, the Mahdi's army of approximately 30,000 wiped out an Egyptian force of 8,000 led by English Colonel William Hicks at Shaykan, also known as El Obeid. This was the capital of Kordofan. Muhammad Ahmad established his own capital there.

GORDON MARCHES INTO THE FIRE

In the face of this revolution, the British government decided to withdraw from Sudan, at least temporarily. It began pulling back its Egyptian-manned armies and government officials. In early 1884 Major General Gordon was sent to Khartoum to usher out the Anglo-Egyptian garrison and residents. About 2,000 occupants of the city—mostly women and children, or injured and ill—were sent downriver. Gordon's mission soon changed from one of evacuation to one of desperate defense, however. Surrounded, Gordon and his Egyptian soldiers apparently could not get out!

Gordon called for reinforcements. If they could hold this strategic city at the confluence of the Nile branches, perhaps all was not lost. Even though they had no hope for the moment of exerting control over the outlying areas (they could not expect to gather taxes and oversee trade while the land was in upheaval), they might keep their grip on this stronghold until the Mahdist movement fizzled. They knew the Mahdi was popular but not invincible. His support was broad and impressive, but he had made some of his officials unhappy. And his nomadic tribes tended to quarrel among themselves. It was only a matter of time, some of the English and Egyptians believed, until the great Mahdist wave would dissipate naturally across the arid sands.

Gordon went so far as to suggest to the British government that Zubayr Pasha, the once-powerful slave trader he had vanquished, be made governor-general of Sudan! It certainly was an unlikely reversal of earlier British objectives. Nevertheless, Gordon proposed, it might undermine the Mahdi's strength. It would offer the masses of Sudanese Arabs another long-popular leader—Zubayr—as a rival to the Mahdi. It might be the only hope. If the Mahdi was not challenged, Gordon believed, his movement could spread to other countries of northeastern Africa. To most of the decision makers in England, however, Gordon's idea seemed preposterous. They said no. They also ignored his repeated urgings for reinforcements.

Historians have debated the true nature of the Khartoum siege. Some believe Gordon was stalling (at least until the final months or weeks of the entrapment), reluctant to abandon such a strategically critical post until it literally was too late for him and his defenders to withdraw. The citizens of England, however, perceived Gordon to be a heroic defender of the crown. They puzzled as month after month passed with no relief expedition being ordered down from Egypt. Queen Victoria herself implored the government to heed Gordon's dispatches for assistance.

By late September 1884 Gordon appeared even to his critics to be genuinely trapped inside Khartoum. British armored steamers coming down the Blue Nile with supplies from Sennar had to brave withering rifle and artillery fire from Mahdist siege forces along the riverbanks before docking at the city. The food and living conditions inside the garrison were becoming deplorable. Gordon, whose journal curiously reflected a sense of humor almost until the very end, wrote that at his dinner table, a mouse "comes up and eats out of my plate without fear."

With telegraph lines cut, Gordon's daring messengers had to finesse their way through the Dervish lines and encampments. Communiques took days, weeks, to deliver. As often as not, they ended up confusing the recipients because of significant fresh events that had transpired while the dispatches were in transit.

THE DEATH OF GORDON

Known as "Chinese" Gordon because of previous service in China, Major General Gordon was one of the western world's most famous and respected military commanders. He first had distinguished himself against the Russians in the Crimean War during the 1850s. His reputation was one of steadfast courage—and perhaps recklessness.

It seems ironic that once Gordon and his force entrenched themselves in Khartoum, the British government practically abandoned them. The military command refused Gordon's request to keep open vital communication links. Certain members of the British government, disappointed and embarrassed by the slavery-marred Egyptian regime, no longer were sure the Mahdist revolt in Sudan was such an evil thing, after all; perhaps the Egyptian regime deserved to lose Sudan!

For months, Gordon's defenders, surrounded by the Mahdi's army, languished. Their situation became desperate. The public outcry to relieve them resulted in a British rescue force finally moving southward from Egypt in October 1884. Lord Garnet Joseph Wolseley commanded. The main part of the expedition was slowed by inept leadership as it labored along the banks of the Nile.

Meanwhile Wolseley sent a "flying column" of 1,600 soldiers mounted on camels across the desert on a direct course to Khartoum. In mid-January 1885, this detachment was attacked furiously by the "Fuzzy Wuzzies," Hadendowa Beja warriors who sided with the Mahdists. The British, though shaken, won the day. But by the time they arrived near Khartoum on January 28, Gordon's unit had been massacred. Gordon was decapitated and his body mutilated (reportedly in violation of the Mahdi's personal orders). For days Khartoum reeked with the odor of rotting corpses. The Mahdists withdrew to their own capital, Omdurman, across the river.

When details of the disaster began to reach England a week later, officials and the public were staggered. Parliament was recessed at the time, and many of the highest government leaders were on holiday, unavailable immediately to determine what Wolseley should do next. As the government stumbled into gear, enraged citizens accused the prime minister, cabinet, and parliament of leaving the hero Gordon to the enemy's pleasure. Queen Victoria wrote in her diary, "All greatly distressed. It is too fearful. The government is alone to blame, by refusing to send the expedition till it was too late."

After agonized deliberation, the British government ordered Wolseley's rescue force to withdraw. There was little his army could do even if it recaptured the city, except wait its own turn for reinforcements. This left not just Khartoum but practically all of Sudan either under the Mahdi's direct control or in his sights.

SUDAN AFTER THE MAHDI

Muhammad Ahmad himself died five months after the fall of Khartoum, apparently of typhus. Following a long power struggle among his lieutenants, Abdallahi ibn Muhammad succeeded him. This man became known as the Khalifah ("deputy").

The Khalifah surprisingly detached himself from the Mahdi's family and long-time supporters. He threw them out of the "Mahyidah" regime, as it had become known, and reorganized the governing entity of northern Sudan. At first, the Khalifah was hopeful of following up the conquest of Khartoum by invading Egypt itself! His armies suffered a series of defeats, however. In southern Egypt, British and Egyptian soldiers beat them back at Tushkah. The Khalifah's forces made progress in an invasion of Ethiopia, but eventually they were repelled in that quarter by Belgians and Italians.

For the next 10 years, the Khalifah ruled a Sudan that became ravaged by as much misery and discontent as ever before. It was a period of brutal tyranny. The Khalifah had some of his own government officials and army officers put to death. The commander Zaki Tamal apparently offended his master not because of ineptitude but because of praiseworthy victories while fighting the Abyssinians; jealous, the Khalifah reportedly had Zaki Tamal sealed alive in a wall. The ruler also hanged his government treasurer, Ibrahim Muhammad Adlan. Some of his political enemies were whipped with thorny switches until they died.

With most of the tribesmen sent off on ceaseless raids, crops went untended. The families they left at home began to starve. When the British eventually decided to retake control of the middle Nile in the 1890s, the Khalifah's weakened military machine was hardly prepared to resist.

Sikh Soldiers, Sudan, 1899 *These Sikh soldiers served under General James Macdonald, who joined General Kitchener's campaign to recapture the Sudan in 1897. Macdonald had been the British commanding officer in Uganda when he was ordered "to push on to Fashoda" to prevent the upper Nile from falling under French domination.*

Macdonald had become impressed with the fighting ability of the Sikhs during his years as an engineer with the British army stationed in India. Macdonald also carried out mapping expeditions in British East Africa—now Kenya and Uganda. While surveying the area for a projected railroad, he mapped previously untraveled mountain passes from East Africa to the Sudan.

6

THE BRITISH RETURN

The people of Great Britain did not forget the massacre of Gordon and his valiant defenders. Sooner or later, many English citizens believed, Gordon must be avenged. Revenge alone, though, was not reason enough to draw British military power to the largely barren middle Nile region. More to the point, Britain began to view Sudan as a vital economic prize. If it could dominate Sudan, it would possess another major piece of the African puzzle. This was a fact the British had realized for generations. If it could not—a possibility that was becoming more and more apparent—then its hold on Egypt might be challenged, and with it, control of the Nile delta and the enormously valuable Suez Canal.

During the 1880s and 1890s, as we have seen, different European nations were focusing their desires to control specific sections of the African continent. In 1884–85, delegates from many European countries met in Berlin to settle among themselves certain established trade domains in Africa and to draw up rules for deciding new trade control zones as the continent continued to "open up" to the outside world.

In this "scramble for Africa," Great Britain was regarded by most rival nations as the logical country to occupy and dominate the lower and middle Nile—Egypt and Sudan. It had to prove itself, though. If England waited too long to exert firm control, another nation might move in and lay claim to parts of the Nile. France and Belgium were the leading contenders.

By the mid-1890s, the British government was debating how and when to go about the "reconquest" of Sudan. Some believed it was more important at the moment to invest British resources in strengthening Egypt's tortured economy by damming the Nile near Aswan. (The first Aswan dam would be built in 1902.) Others turned attentive ears to Italy, which was engulfed in native uprisings of its own in Ethiopia (Abyssinia) to the southeast. Italy claimed the Mahdists had formed an alliance with the Ethiopian rebels, and implored England to invade from the north in order to keep the native union divided and weak. Otherwise, the Italians warned, the whole region might be bloodied in prolonged revolt. The Italians were not merely speculating: An Italian garrison at Kassala on the Sudanese-Ethiopian border was in danger of being overrun by the Dervishes.

KITCHENER'S INVASION

The British began laying their plans. They trained an Egyptian army and organized it according to British designs. The formidable force of almost 26,000, which included more than 8,000 British troops, marched southward into Sudan in March 1896. It was supported by artillery units and by a fleet of River Nile gunboats.

This invading force was led by Herbert Kitchener. Although he was acting officially under the authority of the Egyptian khedive, Kitchener, unlike Gordon a decade before, enjoyed the full, unhalting support of the British government.

Initially, London expected to subdue only the northern part of Sudan. Capturing and securing that much, Parliament believed, was all the English treasury could afford to accomplish along the middle Nile at present. Soon, though, the invasion became far more ambitious. The altered plan was fueled by a growing spirit of expansion, by the lingering desire for revenge, and by fears of French encroachment on the upper Nile. Parliament was further encouraged after Kitchener discovered the Mahdists to be weaker and less organized than expected.

Kitchener took his time reclaiming Sudan. He had rail lines built across the northern Sudanese desert, ensuring a dependable supply of provisions and reinforcements. Between Wadi Halfa and Abu Hamed, the new railroad shortened the previous route between those points along the Nile from two and one half weeks to one and one half days!

One by one during the next two years, Kitchener recaptured the strategic cities and provinces of Sudan: Dongola, a hub of the caravan routes for centuries, Berber, Khartoum, and Fashoda. By the summer of 1898, at least 20,000 natives of the Sudan territory had been killed in the campaign.

The great climactic battle occurred near the desert city of Omdurman, not far from Khartoum on the Nile. The Mahdists sensed this was their final moment. It was early September 1898. The Egyptian-English army was assembled outside Omdurman. The Khalifah threw an army of more than 50,000 against it. But it was a doomed attack—old warfare versus new warfare.

Interestingly, one of the British officers at Omdurman was a wide-eyed, 23-year-old lieutenant destined to become the most famous Briton of the twentieth century. In his diary, he described watching a four-mile-wide sea of Mahdists approach the British-Egyptian position: "The whole side of the hill seemed to move, and the sun, glinting on many hostile spear-points, spread a sparkling cloud." The lieutenant's name was Winston Churchill.

The Mahdists died valiantly, if futilely. Although disillusioned and confused by the destitute living conditions the Khalifah had brought upon their land, they remained faithful to the Mahdi's cause. Their religion taught that to die in battle against the "infidel" Englishman was the ultimate honor. They fought with spears and outdated rifles against Kitchener's machine guns. During the five-hour ordeal at Omdurman, it is estimated some 11,000 charging Muslims fell dead; Kitchener's army lost fewer than 50, with about 400 wounded.

Nazir of the Messeria Tribe, 1900 *The nazir, or sheik, commanded more than 100 men at the Battle of Omdurman (1898). His fighting ability against the Mahdists earned him and his troops the respect of Lord Kitchener. The Messeria live south of Abu Zabad in the Kordofan province. They are one of the nomadic "horse tribes" of the western Sudan. A 1929 description of the aged Nazir was almost rapturous in its description: "Shooting black men and brown men in white robes and white turbans, their spears waving and their bridles of chain flashing in the sunlight, pass in review with their chief at their head. He made a gorgeous figure. A long, beautiful, white sheepskin covered his saddle, while the trappings of his horse were studded with shinning metal. A long blue robe of honor, embroidered in gold and silver, dropped to where it almost covered his feet. A great medal of silver hung among the golden crossblades which fastened his robes to his breast. A snowy white turban was held firmly on his head by a silken cloth bound about head and chin, and from one shoulder, projecting under the armpit, hung a long sword with a hilt of gold. He rode with his chin up, did this old nomad chieftain, and his straight nose, aquiline features, white beard, and white moustache gave him an air of dignity and command."*

KITCHENER—THE NEW HERO

Kitchener's force had no easy campaign. The hardships of the desert and disease took their toll in morale and lives. Stretches of rail line periodically were washed out by Nile flooding. But the cost in Mahdist casualties was many times worse. After one battle, a British officer wrote about a stench of enemy corpses so thick it sickened him.

While systematically eradicating the Mahdists, Kitchener also had to contend in Sudan with a much older rival: France. Fashoda, which we mentioned earlier, was a fortress city on the White Nile several hundred miles south of Khartoum. It was important to France, which was trying to connect its holdings from west to east across sub-Saharan Africa. In July 1898 a small French force commanded by Jean-Baptiste Marchand occupied the fort at Fashoda. Two months later Kitchener's army, driving into southern Sudan, arrived there. Both Marchand and Kitchener were expected to claim Fashoda for their respective governments. The French and English were at a tense impasse. The result of a battle could hardly be in question: Marchand had fewer than 200 men against the British thousands. But was Fashoda even worth fighting over? Was it worth risking a full-blown war between England and France?

The military commanders both swallowed their pride and engaged in wise diplomacy. Three flags rose to flutter above Fashoda: French, British, and Egyptian. Not many weeks afterward, the French foreign minister directed Marchand to pull out of Fashoda. The following year, Britain and France clarified their north African claims in a new agreement. Another detailed piece in the "carving" of Africa by European powers had been defined.

The final outcome of Kitchener's principal campaign against the Dervishes, meanwhile, was a foregone conclusion. In November 1899 the Khalifah was killed in battle. Sudan hardly could mourn his passing; an estimated half of the country's inhabitants died during the Mahdist era, if not in battle then through disease, starvation, and brutality.

Kitchener, who had become idolized in England as the "conqueror of the Sudan," was made a baron and later a viscount

Bugler Boy, 9th Sudanese Battalion, Anglo-Egyptian Nile Expeditionary Force, Omdurman, 1899 *In 1895 the British government authorized Major General Sir Herbert (later Lord) Kitchener to launch a campaign to conquer the Sudan from the Mahdists. The British decision resulted from several international developments, especially conflicting British, French, and Belgian claims at the Nile headwaters. Britain feared that the other colonial powers would take advantage of the Sudan's instability caused by the Mahdist fundamentalist state (1881–98) to move into and occupy the disputed area.*

The Anglo-Egyptian Nile Expeditionary Force included some 26,000 men, 8,600 of whom were British. The remainder were Egyptian units that included six battalions recruited from the southern Sudan. An armed river flotilla escorted the force. The final battle of the campaign occurred on September 2, 1898. The Khalifa, now the leader of the Mahdist state, committed his 52,000-man army to a frontal assault against the Anglo-Egyptian force, which was massed on the plain outside of Omdurman, the Mahdi capital. During the five-hour battle, more than 11,000 Mahdists died. Anglo-Egyptian losses amounted to 48 dead and fewer than 400 wounded. Kitchener then occupied the nearby city of Khartoum, which he rebuilt as the center of the Anglo-Egyptian government in the Sudan.

Many areas of the Sudan welcomed the destruction of the Mahdist state. The Sudanese economy had been all but destroyed during its 19 years of Mahdist rule. The population had dramatically declined because of famine, disease, persecutions, and war. Most of the country's traditional institutions had been shattered—tribes had been divided, and many religious leaders had vanished.

and earl. He went to South Africa to lead British forces in the Boer War, was sent to India as British commander, in 1911 was made proconsul of Egypt, and when World War I began in 1914 was appointed to the British cabinet as secretary of state for war. He succeeded in every role, although he made many enemies and came under public criticism for apparently inhumane tactics, particularly against the Boer guerrillas.

Kitchener died two years into the First World War. A ship on which he was a passenger sank after hitting a German mine off the Scottish coast. It was an ironically cruel ending for one of the most celebrated army commanders of the modern era to die at sea.

SUDAN AT THE CROSSROADS

Back in Sudan, Great Britain was free to focus attention on strengthening its Nile holdings against other European nations. Mahdist factions did not die out altogether, though. Several times in the early 1900s force would be required to put down Mahdist uprisings. As late as 1916 a self-proclaimed prophet named Abd Allah as Suhayni called for a jihad, or holy war, hoping to rally Muslims against the English interlopers in Sudan. These insurgencies had little chance of retaking control of the country, however.

The Mahdist movement is considered by historians to have been the first "nationalist" government of Sudan. Although its legacy was largely one of atrocities and strict authoritarian ideals, the Mahdiyah placed control of Sudan in the hands of natives. After the death of the Khalifah, control of Sudan belonged to Egypt once again—officially. But the British feared that to turn the country's administration over to the Egyptian khedives might lead soon to another debacle as disastrous as the Mahdist rebellion, if not worse. They would not take that risk.

Sudanese Native Officer and Sudanese Interpreter, 1899 *In 1899 the Anglo-Egyptian Condominium created a special political status for the Sudan jointly shared by the khedive of Egypt and Great Britain. However, the Sudan Defense Force was a unique colonial variant with many positive features. Unlike Belgian rule in the Congo, the British trained many Sudanese in military tactics as well as in civil service administration. The British sought to develop an indigenous officer class among educated Sudanese, mostly from influential northern families. Consequently, the Sudan Defense Force came to be viewed as a national organization rather than as an instrument of foreign control.*

Major R.G.T. Bright took this unusual photograph. Bright was one of many British geographers who explored the Sudan and who worked on various boundary commissions. In 1906 the Royal Geographical Society honored Bright for his "various expeditions [which] were of the highest geographical value."

7

THE CONDOMINIUM

England and Egypt came to a rather unusual agreement in January 1899: They would rule newly reconquered Sudan together. This combination of British and Egyptian authority was called a "condominium." It called for the appointment of a governor-general of Sudan who would have "supreme military and civil command."

And who would select the governor-general? The appointment would be made by the khedive, who, you remember, was the "sovereign prince" of the region, chosen and controlled by the Turkish sultan. However, this person was to be picked "on the recommendation of" the British government and could be removed from office only "with the consent of" Britain.

In other words, Great Britain intended to run the country on behalf of the khedive. Kitchener logically was the first governor-general, but he soon was succeeded by another Englishman, Sir Reginald Wingate. Wingate had fought under Kitchener during the years of reconquest and was well acquainted with the country. Among other powers, the governor-general chaired the Executive Council, which was set up in 1910 to oversee the country's law-making and financial matters.

Sheik Yasin Yusif, Gowama Tribe, 1900 *Yasin Yusif was appointed the first civilian administrator of the northern Sudan by the Anglo-Egyptian Condominium in 1900. Having reconquered the Sudan in 1898, the British now had to govern it. But how does an imperial nation administer such a vast land with its varied peoples, customs, and religions? To resolve this dilemma, the Anglo-Egyptian Condominium (1899–1953) was created. Under this agreement, sovereignty over the Sudan was jointly shared by the Egyptian khedive and Great Britain—the Egyptian and British flags would fly side by side throughout the Sudan. The military and civilian government was vested in a governor general appointed by the khedive but nominated by the British. However, from the beginning, Great Britain dominated the condominium. Gradually, civilian administration was restored to the Sudan.*

The first governor general was Lord Kitchener. He was followed by Sir Reginald Wingate (1899–1916). The trust that he gained from the Sudanese people contributed enormously to establishing confidence in Christian British rule of a devoutly Muslim, Arab-oriented people.

HOW THE CONDOMINIUM WORKED

The country was run practically as a British colony. Each Sudanese province had an English governor and administrative staff. Young British administrators came down from England and formed the "Sudan Civil Service." They learned some of the native languages, devised agricultural advances, and oversaw the

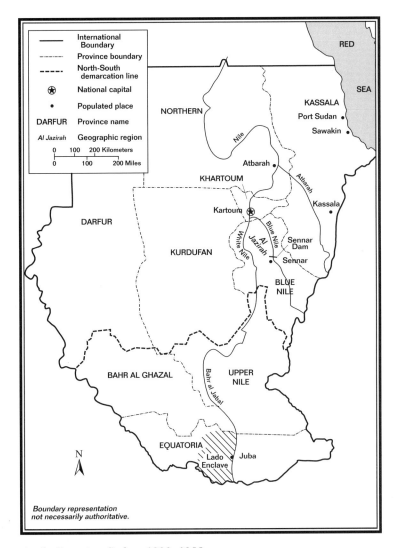

Anglo-Egyptian Sudan, 1899–1955

country's system of law and order. To a limited degree, they became part of the country's social fabric. Below the British officials, Egyptians held less important administrative positions. Below them, in time, native Sudanese were given certain responsibilities.

The British instituted a legal system much like that in India (which in those years was a British colony). At the same time, they recognized the traditional Islamic legal code called the "sharia." The governor-general designated a chief "qadi" as the head of the sharia court system, which had Islamic (Egyptian) administrators and judges.

CONDOMINIUM LIFE IN SUDAN

What was Sudan like at the beginning of the twentieth century? A chronicler named Herbert L. Bridgman offered an interesting description in 1906 when he addressed America's National Geographic Society. It had been just eight years since England had won its "peaceful conquest" of what was known as "Egyptian Sudan." Bridgman reported that "peace, plenty and prosperity reign everywhere. Happiness and content are written on every countenance; life is as safe as in England or in New York. . . ." British rule, he believed, had ushered in a "new era of good times."

Wheat, cotton and sugar cane were Sudan's main crops. Rubber, fruits, ivory, gum, and—interestingly—ostrich feathers also were abundant and valuable exports.

Bridgman's view of prosperity and contentment was not shared by all the natives. During the next half century, they were the ones who would have to deal with problems inherited from their ancestors as well as the strange new challenges of an increasingly industrialized world.

DEFINING A NEW COUNTRY

Although Great Britain had established control over the region, the physical boundaries of Anglo-Egyptian Sudan had not yet been fixed. Treaties with Ethiopia and Belgium set the southeastern and southern borders during the first decade after Kitchener's campaign. The large province of Darfur in the west, though, was not really part of the condominium because it was controlled by the Ottoman sultan Ali Dinar.

The western issue was resolved forcefully after World War I broke out in 1914. Great Britain declared Egypt to be a British protectorate. Ali Dinar became an enemy of England and its war allies because Turkey, the nation to which Ali Dinar owed

Iron-Smelting, Kordofan Province, 1905 *In this photograph ironstone is being heated with charcoal in a cylindrical mud furnace about five feet high and two feet in diameter. The draught, or air draft, is kept up by means of hand-pumped bellows. Smelting takes about 12 hours. The furnace is then broken, and the iron is found in a lump at the bottom.*

Smelting is the process used to turn iron ore into a substance from which products can be made. Hot charcoal is constantly added to the iron ore, reducing it by burning out the impurities. In this primitive process, the end product is a solid lump of iron known as a bloom. A bloom usually weighs about 10 pounds. It consists of pure iron except for some pieces of charcoal. The manufacturing of iron artifacts such as spears required a subsequent shaping operation that involved heating blooms in a fire and hammering the red-hot metal to produce the desired object.

Most iron in the Sudan is mined in the east-central Kassala region between the Atbara River and the Ethiopian border. In 1821 this area was conquered by Egypt. Sixty years later the religious leader al-Mahdi and the Mahdists occupied the Kassala and ruled it until their defeat in 1898 by Anglo-Egyptian forces.

his allegiance, was aligned with Germany, England's great antagonist. A British force took Darfur by force and officially annexed it as part of Sudan. Ali Dinar was killed.

What Great Britain mainly wanted from Sudan during the condominium decades was peace. The British government's real interest lay in Egypt, with its fertile Nile delta and the Suez Canal.

The Sudan region, England reasoned, would provide an effective buffer zone between Egypt and the "scramble" for control that was going on in the African interior and along the east coast.

The Sudanese people, for their part, were divided in their reaction to the condominium. Some showed open resentment to the British and Egyptians alike; some opposed the British but courted alliance with Egypt. Others found places in the condominium system and befriended the British officials. Many tribal peoples, meanwhile, lived essentially as they always had, caring little which foreign power currently claimed control over Sudan as a country.

SLOW PROGRESS

During the first half of the twentieth century, Sudan slowly prospered—in certain areas, at least. The British focused their economic development in the more heavily populated north and along the River Nile. They opened Port Sudan on the Red Sea in 1906 and built additional railroads and telegraph lines north of Khartoum.

In cooperation with a private syndicate, the government in 1911 set about to make the land between the White and Blue Niles a major cotton-producing region. The area was called Jazirah or Gezira, and the cotton venture was known as the Gezira Scheme. During the coming decades, the government built river dams to provide reliable irrigation, opening up more cropland. Soon natives began settling in the Gezira region near Sennar in great numbers. This became a fertile cotton farming area. The produce was sent by train from Sennar to Port Sudan for export to Great Britain and elsewhere.

In the early 1920s Great Britain granted Egypt independence from its "protectorate" status. The British regime in Sudan, however, began pushing the Egyptians from authority in the upper Nile. There was dissension among the Sudanese, some of whom wanted their country to become part of Egypt. Rioting broke out in both Egypt and Sudan. In the midst of the turmoil, Sudan's governor-general, Sir Lee Stack, was assassinated in the Egyptian capital of Cairo. The British response was a

Suk at Nahut (En Nahud), Northern Sudan, 1900 *All Arab cities with some history have their medina. Within the medina are the traditional suks, or markets. There is a feeling of perpetual motion in the suk area of a medina. Craftsmen, sometimes several to a tiny stall, work intently on their tasks. Usually, the smells and sounds from the suks are enthralling—the pungent aroma of mint, spices, wood, and leather. In the suk area, everyone is occupied with his or her own particular work.*

The Prophet Muhammad founded the first Islamic community in a city named Medina, which was second in importance to Mecca. Medina quickly became the prototype of all other towns in the Arab world. To the followers of the Islamic faith, the pursuit of this ideal of the just and ordered city was (and still is) obligatory. It is believed that on the Day of Judgment, men and women will be assessed not only on their own merits but also on their performance in society. Therefore, the design of the medina reflects communal values, each quarter contributing to the benefit of the whole.

demand that every Egyptian public official and soldier leave Sudan. These outcasts were replaced by Sudanese.

Sudan thus came under a form of native bureaucracy known as "indirect rule." British officials were at the top of the government, but tribal and village chiefs were given most of the administrative and judicial responsibilities. Sudan became quite separate from Egypt in the eyes of Great Britain and the world.

Lotuko Men, 1909 *The Lotuko, a people of the extreme southern Sudan, live near Juba in large villages, often of several hundred huts. The Lotuko are a tall, lanky, people with ebony-black bodies. Disdaining clothes because of the heat, they live as hunters, farmers, and herdsmen. Lotuko have their own strict concepts of modesty. To them, kissing is immoral. Men frequently cover their bodies with fine white wood ash and appear like ghostly apparitions. Friends may draw geometric designs in the white coating.*

Most Lotuko villages cling to small hills dotting the flat grasslands. Villages consist of closely grouped circular mud huts, each with a stockade to protect families and goats from wild animals. These villages are semipermanent. In the dry season, many women walk 10 miles daily to muddy holes or creeks for water. The rains regulate the annual cycle of events in a Lotuko village. High, conical grass roofs over thick mud walls keep their houses, or tukls, cool. Wet summer months are devoted to agriculture, dry winter months to hunting.

A "SOUTHERN POLICY" DEVELOPS

In the extreme southern part of the country—the provinces of Bahr al Ghazal and Equatoria, for example—the situation was very different indeed. Communications to and from the villages there continued to be primitive. To the English administrators, there seemed little reason to divert attention and money to that part of the country. In fact, they made southern Sudan off limits to outside visitors. They even closed the southern area to northern Sudanese and forbade northerners from going there to work.

Yet slave trading continued there and in certain other areas even after the condominium government was established. The British were obliged to deal with it. And as for ages past, there were tribal wars to be contained in remote parts of the sprawling country. Aside from this necessary policing, southern Sudan essentially was ignored by the British.

In retrospect, the "hands-off" approach by the English administrators seems to have been both bad and good for southern Sudan: bad in the sense that brutal tribal ways, which included slave trading and other customs that appeared savage to the European administrators, were continuing into the twentieth century; good in the sense that important native traditions of a less offensive nature were left alone, unspoiled by the Europeans.

The British encouraged southern autonomy (self-rule), in fact. In 1930 an official decree tended to set the southern native blacks apart from the northern Arabs. Ultimately, many British administrators believed, southern Sudan and its people should be enfolded into British East Africa, the English colonies down along the continent's eastern coast. Lifestyles, cultures, and traditions there were a world apart from the Arabized north of Africa. Down the coast, many Europeans reasoned, was where the natives of southern Sudan should be pigeonholed.

Ambitious Arabs in the south wielded a certain degree of control over trading around the upper Nile. (In time the Arab merchants would be ushered from the southern region.) Presbyterian and Anglican missionaries provided medical services and schools here and there. A few of their graduates went on to college, but usually in the surrounding European colonies, not at Sudan's own higher learning facilities in Khartoum.

These practices symbolized the distinctions that had been drawn between northern and southern Sudan. As the country looked toward independence in the mid-twentieth century, the distinctions would become more pronounced. Soon enough, the divisiveness would erupt in civil war.

Lotuko Woman, 1909 *Lotuko women consider skin scarification a sign of beauty. "Beauticians" jab a sharp curved pin into the skin, pull it to a point, and slice off the tip. When the design is completed, oily ocher is rubbed over the cuts to cause bleeding. These skin scars denote age—but only imagination governs the varied designs. Many women have a hole punctured just beneath their lower lip in which they wear a stick.*

Unmarried Lotuko girls wander about a village completely naked or wearing a meager row of thin chains dangling from a narrow beaded belt. Tribal laws forbid men from touching these "iron curtains." Married women replace the chains with goatskin skirts.

The Lotuko staple food is a soupy millet porridge. They drink a very low-alcoholic beer made from durra, a sorghum grain. Corn grows poorly because of the irregular rainfall. However, peanuts thrive and provide a welcome food before grains ripen. Although most Lotuko have large herds of goats, these flocks are left to breed instead of being butchered, as they are the chief wealth of a family.

Lotuko Hunters, 1909 *Hunters carry long spears that have been sharpened on smooth rocks. The men, their spears held high, circle around their quarry. Then the human trap closes in—killing a lion, gazelle, jackal, or even a buffalo. In the face of danger, group discipline is well maintained. For example, if a Lotuko is faced with a buffalo charge, he will fall prone, knowing that the buffalo cannot swing his massive horns near the ground. A prostrate hunter who then thrusts his spear upward into the advancing animal's neck becomes a village hero. Elephant meat is considered a delicacy. When an elephant is killed, hundreds of screaming, blood-soaked Lotuko tear at every bit of flesh and bone.*

Rainmakers are extremely respected in Lotuko society. Rain brings flying hoards of fat, winged termites, much relished by the Lotuko. Lured by flames and caught in pits especially dug to collect them, these insects are eaten raw or coated with honey.

The north-south tension even spread among British government officials. Administrators in the north opposed calls for money to improve conditions in the south; they thought it would be wasted. British officials in the south, meanwhile, were prejudiced against the Arab-dominant north. This kind of festering pressure at every level could hardly lead to anything but an explosive release. The explosion would not come, though, until after independence.

Natives at Kusti, 1919 *With a few exceptions, all major Sudanese towns lie along one of the Niles. One of the most striking characteristics of the Sudan is the diversity of its people. The Sudanese are divided among some 19 major ethnic groups and almost 600 subgroups. They speak more than 100 languages and dialects.*

A major cleavage exists between the northern and the southern parts of the country. The north is dominated by Muslims, most of whom speak Arabic and identify themselves as "Arabic"—about 39 percent of the population in 1956. In the south, the people are "Africans" who, for the most part, follow traditional African religions. The largest non-Arab group is the Dinka. (The only census in Sudanese history that recorded ethnicity was taken in 1956.) However, those Sudanese who consider themselves Arab are, for the most part, racially mixed and usually are indistinguishable from black southerners. Despite a common religion and language, Sudanese Arabs are not a cohesive group.

8

INDEPENDENCE

Compared with the centuries of invasion and slave raiding that came before and the decades of civil strife that would follow independence, Sudan was a relatively peaceful place under the British-Egyptian condominium. But there were disputes, especially concerning land ownership—a vital issue in a country where most land is desert or barren plain.

Mekki Abbas, an Arab born in a village near the Blue Nile, became a scholar, teacher, newspaper editor, and government official during the condominium years. In his book, *The Sudan Question*, published several years before independence, Abbas described the legal state of affairs in northern Sudan:

> The magistrates of Wadi Halfa district may go for 10 or 20 years without having to try a case of murder or of grievous bodily hurt. But much litigation goes on about land. A case about a fraction of an acre or two palm-trees may run into volumes and take years to decide. This is due to the scarcity of arable land which also causes a heavy migration of labour to Egypt or to the interior of the Sudan.

EARLY SEEDS OF DISCONTENT

There was a more significant reason for unrest during the condominium years. Despite cooperation, there never had been a genuine bond between Sudanese and Egyptian natives and the English non-Muslims who held much of the national power. When the British-led army went south to reconquer Sudan from the Mahdists in the late 1890s, some Egyptian citizens and government administrators hoped the campaign would fail. This was ironic, since Sudan was being retaken (in principle, at least) on behalf of the Egyptian government. Great Britain, of course, had its own national interests at stake in the campaign—interests that were obvious to suspicious Arabs. Egyptian officials realized Kitchener's defeat of the Mahdists was a victory more for England than for Egypt.

The Turkish Empire, which manipulated the Egyptian khedives, also was alarmed by Kitchener's reconquest. Here was an army consisting largely of Egyptian Muslims, invading a Muslim-held land. There were diplomatic protests and even a threat by the Turkish sultan to interfere against Kitchener's invasion force. The British government fended off the opposition, partly with diplomatic assurances that the military expedition was in the sultan's best interests and partly by flexing its naval muscle in the Mediterranean. Any Turkish force sent to interfere in Sudan clearly would be opposed.

By then, of course, Turkey held only feeble authority in Egypt and none at all in Mahdist-controlled Sudan. The controversy died out, and Kitchener's army proceeded to win its campaign rather easily. But Arab resentment of European power in northern Africa grew deeper. Shortly after the reconquest, when the British and Egyptians formed their condominium to govern Sudan, the region appeared stabilized and happy to the watching world. Behind the public window, however, was a festering discontent.

AFRICANS SEEK SELF-GOVERNMENT

As in other African "protectorates," a spirit of nationalism grew in Egypt and Sudan during the first half of the twentieth century, especially after World War I. Natives became better educated and naturally wondered why they couldn't—and shouldn't—govern themselves.

In Sudan, the spirit of nationalism began to flourish in the north among the Muslims who resented Britain's "indirect rule." They believed the English administrators deliberately were dividing the country, north from south. Sudan should become united and independent, they decided, with Khartoum the capital. These new nationalists were agreed in their underlying objective but divided as to how to go about it. There was little question among them that Sudan should become self-governing. At issue was whether native administrators in the British-controlled government should acquire control gradually or whether the Sudanese people should rise in force and drive out the British all at once—perhaps with the help of Egypt. Many people yearned for independence from Great Britain, but not necessarily for independence from Egypt.

In 1924, Sudan Governor-General Sir Lee Stack was assassinated. This naturally led to a season of tension throughout Sudan while the British decided how to react and reassert control. At the time, a former Muslim army officer named Ali Abd al Latif was promoting Sudanese independence through a political organization called the United Tribes Society (later called the White Flag League). Ali Abd al Latif was arrested during the postassassination turmoil. In response, an army unit mutinied. The mutiny was put down, and Sudan's first active effort toward nationalism fizzled.

Neverless, the spirit of nationalism grew in Sudan. A decade later, educated natives increasingly were questioning the powers of the British governor-general and his lieutenants. They wanted an independent Sudanese nation—or at least, a joint Egyptian-Sudanese nation, independent of the British. But there were complications. For example, even the British government officials who favored eventual Sudanese independence believed they were *helping* the natives, not *dominating* them. A very real concern existed, rooted in history, of what measures the Egyptians might take in Sudan if the British pulled out. Some English condominium officials truly thought they were doing the Sudanese a great favor—at their personal inconvenience and peril—by shepherding Sudan clear of Egyptian dominion.

Some natives agreed. At best, it appeared to them, independence would divide the country: Northern Sudan quickly would become part of Egypt, while southern Sudan would become affiliated with the central or eastern African nations. This result was abhorrent to most nationalists of the period. Their objective was a united, independent Sudan, not a division that would annex some areas of Sudan to one bordering country and other areas to other countries.

THE POLITICS OF INDEPENDENCE

When World War II broke out across Europe and, in due course, northern Africa, Italian soldiers, allied with Nazi Germany (Britain's archrival), invaded southeastern Sudan from their Ethiopian stronghold. They met iron resistance from Sudan's native army, the Sudan Defense Force (SDF). Not only that: the SDF, uniting with British troops, soon pushed the infiltrators back and wrested Ethiopia from Italian hands.

During the war, a political group known as the Graduates' General Conference demanded an end to north-south separatist policies. They wanted to see more native Sudanese appointed to government service and, ultimately, a self-governing Sudan. Their demands weren't accepted immediately, but the British administrators by now saw the handwriting on the wall—the condominium years clearly were numbered. High British officials in Sudan were recommending a unified government for both north and south. The condominium's old Executive Council was replaced in 1948 with a Legislative Assembly, which partly consisted of elected members. The "closed door" policy in southern Sudan ended.

We might think of these as significant steps toward unification and independence, but not all Sudanese did. The Legislative Assembly was opposed by the powerful Ashigga, or National Unionist Party (NUP). The NUP was a political orga-

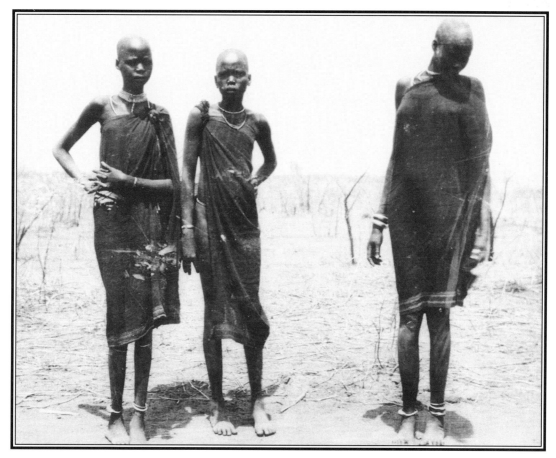

Dinka Girls, 1935 *A Dinka girl is expected to identify more with her father than her mother—although it is through her mother that she learns to be a wife. Her main family contribution is to attract bridewealth, which her brothers and other male relations will use for their own marriages. Through marriage, she also widens the circle of relatives. Yet the Dinka speak of girls as "slaves" to be "sold" and a "stranger" who will "leave" her own kin for another. Without a doubt, girls in a Dinka family are subordinate to their brothers.*

nization that wanted to see Sudan and Egypt united as one nation. It boycotted the Legislative Assembly because it distrusted the ability or motivation of that assembly to accomplish the unification goal. The boycott may have been a valiant gesture in the eyes of some, but it left control of the Legislative

Assembly in the hands of NUP opponents—most notably, the factions that wanted Sudan to become an independent nation, separate from Egypt.

Certain British administrators in the south, meanwhile, encouraged the idea of regional division. They predicted that an independent Sudan placed under the control of northern Muslims would become a Sudan bound for sectional rebellion. Natives in the south tended to agree. Their forecast, tragically, would prove correct.

THE NATIONALIST DREAM COMES TRUE . . . AT A PRICE

In 1953 England and Egypt set up a trial period of self-government for Sudan. Interestingly, the NUP faction won considerable popular control during the transition period. The temporary Sudanese government of 1954 came under the leadership of Ismail al Azhari, the NUP leader.

Friction between north and south already was escalating. Southern Sudanese were appalled when Arabic was made the official language of the trial government. It meant few native southerners—even those who'd graduated from the mission schools—were likely to receive administrative appointments, because they did not speak Arabic. Worse, familiar local officials in the southern region began to be replaced almost exclusively with Arabic-speaking northerners whom the people distrusted.

This distrust turned to violence. In August southern Sudanese soldiers were infuriated when transfers placed them under the thumbs of northern commanders. They mutinied. Several hundred government officials, army officers, and others were killed. Some 70 mutineers were caught and put to death. Other rebel soldiers fled to the hills and villages and began organizing opposition to the Arab government. This was the beginning of guerilla warfare that would ravage the south for many years to come.

By 1955 Azhari realized most of the Sudanese people wanted a separate Sudan, not a union with Egypt. He therefore changed his political stance and advocated independence. Late that year Sudan's parliament voted to create a Sudanese republic, independent of foreign dominion. Their resolution took effect January 1, 1956. Sudan had become a nation!

But were Sudan's ages of discord coming to a glorious end . . . or about to explode?

Arab Sheik, Central Sudan, 1909 *In the Arab world, a sheik is the head man of a village or tribe. The term is also applied to learned men, especially to theologians and to anyone who has memorized the Koran, however young he might be.*

9

A NATION DIVIDED

The governor-general no longer was Sudan's head of state. Sudan now had its own parliament, with a house of representatives elected by popular vote and a senate elected indirectly. The parliament chose a Supreme Commission of five individuals to run the administration. A prime minister, nominated by the house and confirmed by the Supreme Commission, also was placed in office.

The first few years of independence were especially tense. In the south, both Christian and pagan natives were unhappy with the new republic's government, which was controlled by Muslims. Meanwhile, many people feared that Egypt, now that Great Britain had removed itself from the picture, might send an army to bring the upper Nile within its domain.

Agricultural and economic problems arose as well. The country was dependent on cotton as its only major export crop. In 1957 the cotton crop was extremely good—too good. So much cotton was available to the world market that prices dropped lower and lower. The low prices may have been a happy development for foreign consumers, but they were a calamity for cotton producers. And the next year Sudan's cotton farmers faced the opposite problem: a dismal harvest.

THE GOVERNMENT FALLS

Several strong political parties were fighting grimly for control of the new government, making the political atmosphere quite unstable. Azhari's administration fell apart in 1956. A former army commander named Abd Allah Khalil became head of a coalition government.

In 1958 Khalil conspired with Sudanese army officials and leaders of one of the main political groups to seize military control of the government. General Ibrahim Abbud became the military government leader. At first Abbud's regime did well on the strength of a rebounding cotton crop. Abbud was not a skillful statesman, however. In the coming years, he found himself under increasing criticism for his overall economic and educational policies.

Dissension festered within the military itself, aggravated by such political factions as the Sudanese Communist Party and a labor-based group called the United National Front. And in the south, groups of guerrillas called collectively the Anya Nya began carrying out acts of rebellion. Fortunately for Abbud, the Anya Nya were unable to mount a major revolt because they were divided along religious and ethnic lines.

It was nine years before a civilian government returned to power. In a relatively peaceful changeover in late 1964, Abbud disbanded the military regime. Labor and army leaders chose a temporary prime minister. The next year, elections were held, placing Muhammad Ahmad Mahjub at the head of another coalition government. Mahjub, in turn, was ousted a year later, and Sadiq al Mahdi gained enough factional support to become prime minister.

Such was the unstable state of affairs that for a time in 1968 Sudan found itself with two rival government administrations. One group convened on the lawn outside the parliament building while the other functioned inside! Soon, after indecisive elections, Mahjub regained control of Sudan's government as prime minister—but again, not for very long.

In the meantime the Sudanese army occupied southern Sudan. In their zeal to put down guerilla activities, the soldiers reportedly went to extremes, burning civilians' homes, churches, schools, and crops. In this region of Sudan, many natives were leaving the cities and taking to the bush country. Some were relocating to adjoining countries. Sudan, dominated by its northern Muslim population, thus was becoming more Arab-speaking and Arab-thinking, rather than "African."

Nimeiri's Rise to Power

Establishment of a firm civilian government for Sudan seemed hopeless. In May 1969 an army colonel named Jaafar an Nimeiri organized a successful military coup. Nimeiri believed a return to military authority was past due. The country's political fragmentation and the refusal of major parties to cooperate made it impossible for Sudan to solve its growing problems, he reasoned. He became head of a unique system of government that, although chronically shaky, was to become the longest-lasting regime of independent Sudan.

Nimeiri established himself as chairman of a Revolutionary Command Council that did away with all prior government institutions and outlawed political parties. The council appointed Babikr Awadallah, a leading presidential candidate before the coup, to run the government as prime minister. Oddly, Awadallah oversaw a cabinet that included Nimeiri himself as minister of defense. Awadallah had been supported politically by Sudanese communists and other left-wing factions, and his cabinet now was composed heavily of communist and Marxist officials.

Perhaps even more strangely, within a matter of months, Awadallah was removed from his post—yet continued to serve on the Revolutionary Command Council as foreign minister. Nimeiri became prime minister.

Fighting broke out the next year between government forces and soldiers of the conservative Ansar movement. The Ansar and their leader had established a stronghold on Aba Island in the Nile (where a century before the Mahdi had planted the seeds of his revolution). Some 3,000 Sudanese died when Nimeiri's army launched a massive assault on the island. Aba Island was captured, and the Ansar leaders were killed or scattered.

Nimeiri then took steps to break up the powerful communist organization in the country. In retaliation, communists attempted a coup and momentarily captured Nimeiri and the Revolutionary Command Council. Nimeiri's army leaders, however, quickly put down the coup and restored him to power. Nimeiri in 1971 was elected president and proclaimed Sudan to be a "socialist democracy."

CONTINUING STRIFE IN THE SOUTH

Throughout these years of government instability in Khartoum, southern Sudanese had existed in constant fear. After 15 years of struggle, an estimated half million people had died in southern Sudan. Rebels, hiding and operating from the wild bush country, fought against government troops. While Sudan's government military was obtaining weapons from the Soviet Union, the southern guerillas were being supplied by Israel and sympathetic organizations in different parts of Africa and abroad.

Joseph Lagu ultimately became the leader of the southern rebels, forming the Southern Sudan Liberation Movement (SSLM). Nimeiri chose to avert all-out war with him, if possible, and tried to negotiate an end to the fighting. In 1972 government and SSLM representatives met in neighboring Ethiopia to see if an agreement could be forged that would protect southern interests, short of creating a separate state in that region. Ethiopian Emperor Haile Selassie played a key role in bringing about an eventual accord, which was signed in March 1972.

To an extent, southern Sudan gained its own self-government. A Southern Regional Assembly was to be elected. The assembly would nominate a "president" of the southern provinces; this regional president's actual appointment, however, would be made official by the president of Sudan. Everyday affairs in the south would be governed by a High Executive Cabinet, its members appointed by the regional president.

The south also gained control, to a great extent, over its own division of the nation's army. And it was allowed to make English

Nuer Village, 1921 *The Nuer people live in the marshy area on both banks of the Nile River in the southern Sudan. Because their land is flooded for part of the year and parched for the rest of it, they spend the rainy season in permanent villages built on higher ground and the dry season in riverside camps. The treeless flat land where the Nuer live is so trampled upon by elephants in the wet season that thousands of deep holes—their footmarks—cover the entire area.*

The Nuer are a long-legged people with the unique customs of plastering their hair with red mud and of keeping count of love affairs by making scars on their body. It is not uncommon to see Nuer men with their bodies painted white and their face and neck colored a brilliant red. Another Nuer fashion is that of smearing the body with butter, which gives it a beautifully polished black shine.

A 1906 American adventure traveler noted that the vanity of the Nuer was "amazing." "I saw two men with brass bracelets so tight round the forearm that the circulation had almost ceased and the hands had got swollen and almost atrophied. In two cases which came under my observation these bracelets had actually cut into the flesh of the wrist. When I asked why they did not remove them, as the hand was getting absolutely paralyzed, they said they would rather lose the use of their hands altogether than remove such a becoming ornament."

its primary regional language, although Arabic remained the official language of Sudan. Ultimately, though, the south still would be part of Sudan. It would be subject to national decisions in such matters as the overall economy, national defense, and international affairs.

UNREST IN BOTH NORTH AND SOUTH

To encourage unity among the northern Arab-dominated factions, Nimeiri and his government acknowledged Islam as the official religion of Sudan and the Islamic sharia as the basis for lawmaking. He faced continued strong opposition from Muslim conservatives. Unsuccessful coups were attempted, sometimes entailing fatal violence and invariably followed by numerous arrests and political purges.

There followed a decade of radically changing approaches to leadership by Nimeiri. At first, he actively and publicly sought "national reconciliation" with his enemies, released hundreds of political prisoners, and even allowed them to run for office in the 1978 elections. The result was the weakening of Nimeiri's official national party, the Sudan Socialist Union. Corruption among government officials infuriated the citizens. Nimeiri responded to the growing discontent with repression, hoping strong-arm tactics would stabilize his control. He had thousands of political enemies locked up and replaced many of his government and military leaders with personal friends—individuals who were not particularly qualified for those duties.

Soon, fearing renewed upheaval in the south, Nimeiri disbanded the Southern Regional Assembly and divided that region into its traditional provinces. Rebel groups resumed their often violent acts of resistance. During the 1980s, some 3 million southern Sudanese were driven from their homes, and more than a million people died from fighting and famine.

In the north there were strikes and riots as a result of worsening economic factors. Nimeiri's troubles reached a climax in April 1985. In the face of rising prices, heavy international debt, southern strife, political turmoil, and opposition to the sometimes brutal punishments (amputation and death) of the sharia system, military officers seized control of the government and sent Nimeiri into exile. They were unable to alleviate the country's underlying problems, but they permitted open activities by different political parties. A year later, they held popular elections.

Al-Bashir Becomes Leader

Sadiq al Mahdi emerged from the voting as head of a coalition government. He was unable to cope effectively with the country's ills and dissensions. Famine ravaged southern Sudan, adding to his troubles. After three years of disjointed rule, he was ousted in another military coup, and Colonel Umar Hassan Ahmad al-Bashir took control of the country.

Al-Bashir, like Nimeiri, outlawed political parties in Sudan. He set up a military council to run the country. This council in 1993 appointed him president. Three years later, elections were held to create a new parliament; Al-Bashir was elected to continue as president. Control of parliament went to the National Islamic Front, a group rooted in the Islamic legal tradition. Predictably, non-Muslim rebels in the south have continued their guerilla campaign to the present day.

Officially Sudan today is a republic with a president (Al-Bashir) as its chief of state, supported by a cabinet appointed by the president. Laws are made by the country's 400-member National Assembly. The president and assembly representatives serve elected terms.

Shilluks, c. 1900 *The Shilluk community is a cluster of hamlets with a chief chosen by the elders. Historically, these hamlets have been united by the reth, the divine-right king who is chosen from the sons of previous kings.*

10

THE PEOPLE OF SUDAN

The people who have come together during many centuries in what is modern-day Sudan are notably diverse. Dark-skinned Africans have moved in from the south. Arabs have invaded from the Asian continent to the northeast. Greek and Roman armies briefly overran parts of Egypt to the north, and elements of their cultures rippled into the Sudan area. More recently, English explorers and other Europeans tried to exert control and, in doing so, brought their own cultural and governmental influences to bear on Sudan.

The country has absorbed all these human elements. Listening to the national anthem of Sudan without knowing the origin of the music, you might think you were hearing a bit of European classical music. Listening to a folksinger like Hamza El Din, on the other hand, you might think you were in Arabia. Accompanying himself on a native stringed instrument called an oud, Hamza during the 1960s brought to western society a taste of balladry from his native Nubia, the ancient region of northern Sudan and southern Egypt.

A GEOGRAPHIC MELTING POT

As we've seen, Sudan is a country where Africa meets Arabia. This effect of culture upon culture is not just intercontinental, but "intra"-continental. If we examine the histories and traditions of the different peoples of Sudan such as the Nuba people of Central

Natives at Kusti, 1919 *Kusti, the site of this photograph, is a town in the central Sudan. Located on the western bank of the White Nile, it is about 65 miles south of El-Dueim (Ad-Duwaym) and 180 miles south of Khartoum. Population is an estimated 75,000 today. Oil discoveries in the area led to the 1981 decision to construct a refinery at Kusti. This refinery has a limited output, and it can barely meet a fraction of the Sudan's overall petroleum requirements.*

Sudan, we see that each has influenced—and been influenced by—its neighbors. Over a period of centuries, neighboring and invading people have intermarried. They have adopted new customs, rituals, and beliefs.

The powerful Egyptians to the north invaded Nubia seeking building materials for the great Egyptian royal courts and tombs, and slaves to transport these materials and provide labor. One result of these invasions was a mingling of cultures. Cultural

Nuba People, Central Sudan, 1904 *The Nuba live in the Nuba hills of the Kordofan region of the central Sudan, some 300 miles south of Khartoum. At the turn of the twentieth century, they numbered about 300,000. All are called Nuba, although they are split into some 50 tribes of varying size. Some have more than 20,000 members, others fewer than 1,000. Each tribe speaks its own dialect. These many speech patterns have baffled linguists who have attempted to clarify their various language groups. (The Nuba are from the Kordofan, whereas the Nubians are from the Nile valley of Khartoum.)*

In general, the Nuba are peaceful people. The men learn to be expert spear handlers, but this tradition dates back to the days when a tribe was forced to protect itself against marauders. In most tribal fights, which are usually over women, sticks and not spears are the chosen weapons.

Two Men, Darfur Area, c. 1920 *During 1919–20, Philip Brockle-hurst followed the Muslim pilgrim route across central Africa from the Red Sea to Lagos on the west coast. This well-traveled route was used by Muslims enroute to and from Mecca. He photographed these two men in the western Darfur region of the Sudan near the border with Chad. Brocklehurst, a noted explorer, had accompanied Ernest Shackleton on his 1907 expedition to Antarctica. He also was the first to reach the summit of Mount Erebus, a 14,000-foot active volcano on the Ross Island formation in the Antarctic region.*

influences worked both ways. While Egyptians exerted strong influences on the Nubians they conquered, the Nubian slaves took their artistic and religious influences into Egypt. It has been through Sudan that Egypt over the centuries has absorbed its strongest African features.

Here along the Nile we see perhaps as clearly as anywhere else on the globe how geography affects culture. A region's geographic features (water sources, croplands, wildlife, natural resources) attract its neighbors from different directions. Certain of these neighboring peoples may come in and conquer the region—or, if

Amhara Family, Sudan-Ethiopia Border, 1901 *The Amhara are descendants of ancient Semitic conquerors of Ethiopia. Today, they are members of the Ethiopian Orthodox Church, a religion preserved virtually intact from the fifth century A.D. All but one of Ethiopia's emperors from 1270 to 1974 were Amhara.*

they lack military prowess, may simply settle. They might intermingle with those who already are there, or live close by, separate but generally peaceful. The newcomers bring their customs, languages, religions, and forms of government with them.

One example of this cross-influencing occurred during the sixteenth century B.C., when Egypt hired Nubian soldiers to help defend Egypt against Hyksos invaders from Asia. These mercenaries ("soldiers of fortune") from the south introduced elements of their culture among their Egyptian allies and took home with them some of the customs they had learned in Egypt.

Peoples from the west (modern-day Libya and Chad) moved into the Nile region and as far eastward as the Red Sea. They, too, became part of the culture of ancient Sudan. For many centuries, merchants transported goods by camel caravan through the Sahara Desert.

Dinka Girls Pounding Grain, 1904 *Dinkas also are cultivators. However, their grain production is generally poor in quantity. This has to do with their primitive implements and the harsh climate—both of which limit the amount of land that can be tilled. For example, so unpredictable is the climate that when it does rain, the people plant, but an extensive dry period may follow, during which the crops die. Conversely, torrential downpours may occur, drowning the seedlings. Worms, locusts, birds, and all sorts of animals also threaten crops.*

The Dinka always are in direct contact with a hostile environment. The blazing sun of the dry season kills the grass. The soil dries, forming wide and deep crevices. Swarms of restless flies torment both man and beast. The wet season brings heavy rains. The Nile and its tributaries overflow, leaving floods, swamps, and mud. Lions, leopards, hyenas, wild dogs, buffalo, crocodile, snakes, and scorpions pose a continuous threat.

But the Dinka love their country. They are self-sufficient: they have cattle, and the rivers teem with fish. Moreover, there are many wild vegetables and fruits. Depending on the season, the skies are filled with birds of every color. The fields swarm with butterflies. These people believe that they are living in total harmony with nature.

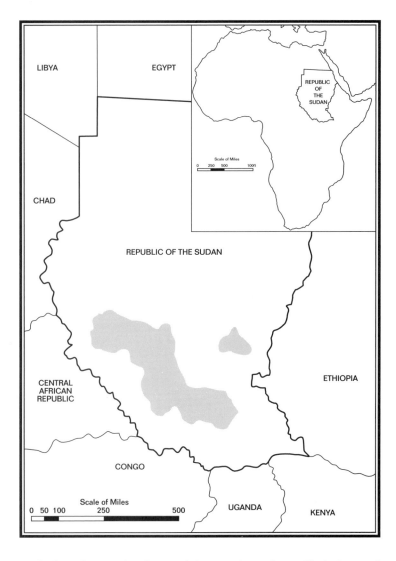

The Dinka of the Sudan.

Sudan also, we've learned, is a region where Christian and Muslim influences have converged. In Khartoum today, you will find churches, cathedrals, and mosques serving Roman Catholic, Coptic Christian, Greek, Ethiopian Orthodox, Anglican (English Protestant), and Muslim worshipers. You also will find people of the Maronite faith. These believers use a notably Eastern form of worship and church discipline but recognize the Roman Catholic pope's authority.

Two Dinkas (with Tall Hats) and Two Arabs, at Renek, White Nile, 1903 *The Dinka are a non-Moslem people. Long before nineteenth-century colonialism, enmity existed between the Negroid South and the Arab North. This hatred, caused by Arab slave raids, caused the Dinka to reject Arab culture.*

A contemporary authority on Dinka life recalls that as a child "we were still frightened into silence by such exclamations as 'There come the camels.' The expectation was that the Arabs would capture and put [us] in their large skins on the sides of their camels." Nevertheless, leading Arab and Dinka families always were in diplomatic contact as friendly neighbors.

Although the Dinka fought against Turko-Egyptian domination, the fundamentalist Mahdist regime (1881–1898) brought terror to them. Under British rule (1899–1955), all peoples were lumped together into a loose unity but otherwise were kept separate and independent. This British "Southern Policy" of divide-and-rule further contributed to the fragmentation of the Sudan. With independence in 1955, the promised confederation of the north and the south on equal terms never materialized.

This photograph was taken by Captain H. H. Wilson, who spent several years in the upper Nile region above Fashoda. Wilson, an expert surveyor, was assigned by the Anglo-Egyptian Condiminium in 1900 to map designated areas.

Reth, Shilluk King, 1899 *The Shilluk king, or reth, is at front-center of this photograph. The king is responsible for the morality and well-being of his people. By tradition, and until the early twentieth century, the king was put to death in a ritualistic ceremony if he became weak or senile. Diedrich Westermann, an American missionary from the Board of Foreign Missions of the United Presbyterian Church of North America was able to publish a short grammar of the Nilotic Shilluk language in 1912. (It is estimated that more than 130 languages are spoken in the Sudan.) The Board of Foreign Missions has been working on a translantion of the entire Bible into Shilluk.*

Shilluk Dancers, 1935 *Shilluk dance is a celebration of their first king, Nyikang. They dance wearing masks fashioned from gourds with applied facial features made from cattle dung and fishbone teeth. They believe God orders everything—including misfortune and death. Each Shilluk must reconcile the goodness and justice of God with the observable facts of evil and suffering. Some anthropologists consider the Shilluk religion to be linked to the Hebrew concept of monotheism.*

Generally, Arab elements today pervade northern Sudan. Most northern Sudanese are Muslims and speak forms of Arabic, although their languages are not identical to those of the Arabic-speaking Mediterranean coastal countries. In all, about half the total population of Sudan are Arabs—easily the country's largest ethnic group. A variety of black African peoples have dominated the southern third of the country. More diversified, they speak many languages and practice different native religions. Christianity also is common in southern Sudan. The southern Dinka are the largest group of black Africans in Sudan.

Shilluk Dancers, 1901

Old Customs Survive

Primitive customs and rituals—some of them alarming to westerners—have continued into modern times among some of the rural people. Into the twentieth century they included human sacrifice. As recently as 1926, H. C. Jackson, one of the condominium governors, reported an encounter between a government forestry inspector and Azande natives in southern Sudan. Walking through the jungle, the inspector, identified by the governor as "R.," was startled by shrieks in the distance.

Shilluks, 1903 *The Shilluks are unique among the Nilotic peoples in that they are the only peoples of this group with a strong central government, the dynasty of which dates back to the early sixteenth century. Anthropologists know that during that period, Hamitic invaders from the east swept down on the Nilotes. These Hamites may have introduced monotheism to the Shilluks, indeed a most interesting occurrence in the history of religion.*

Following the sound of the commotion, he and his servant-bearers entered a clearing where a crowd of natives had gathered.

> The men, some with their heads completely shaved, or with a parting carefully cut down the middle, others with plaits adorned with a feather, wore the usual skirt of bark; they were drunk with banana beer and mad with excitement. The women were naked except for a bunch of leaves in front and behind, suspended from a fibre string around their waists; they, like the men, were infected by some deep emotion. But it was fear and horror that were depicted upon their faces, not the ferocious blood-lust that transfigured the men into creatures frenzied and obscene. Alone, but for a few terrified carriers, the Inspector made straight for the middle of the throng, despite the angry

Nuba Wrestlers, Kordofan, 1904 *These Nuba wrestlers were photographed in the town of Jebel el Aheima in the Kordofan region of the central Sudan.*

The Nuba stress development of strength and courage in their young men chiefly by training them for wrestling. Intervillage matches are peaceful affairs accompanied by the beating of drums and culminating in a huge feast.

To ward off evil, men bathe in white wood ash before any physical sport. The ash also helps an opponent to get a grip on an otherwise slippery body.

From the time a Nuba boy reaches manhood, he is trained in wrestling. Before his first bout, his father gives him white scarves, which are tied around his neck and waist. Elaborate ceremonies mark his promotion to more strenuous matches with wrestlers from other villages. He now receives a cow's tail from his father, new scarves cut from colored cloth, and a goatskin belt. Older men stage a practice bout to teach the finer points of the sport. From a brother of his mother, he receives a bull to signify his "coming of age." If the young man wins a bout, he can add brass bells and monkey fur to his waist band.

Often a young wrestler, after winning, is lashed viciously across the chest by an older man. This is believed to make the youth stronger. The stunned boy attempts to show his strength by walking unaided from the ring.

protests of the crowd, and saw a large open pit some four feet across. At the bottom was the trussed body of the dead Sultan surrounded by calabashes of food and drink, and beside the pit R. saw some young girls whose screams had first attracted his notice. R. asked the Sultan's son—a brutal, truculent young man—what had caused these screams and shrieks. The youth explained that when a great chief died, young girls had to accompany him into the world beyond the grave to minister to his wants. "This," said the Sultan's son, "is the custom of my people and I will carry it out whatever you or your government says or threatens; the legs of these girls will now be broken and the girls will be thrown into the grave and buried alive with my dead father." R., alone though he was, and faced with a mob half mad with fanatic exaltation, ordered the ceremony to stop. The Sultan's son raved and fumed; R. stood calm and resolute. . . .

The narrative—doubly notable because it depicted the tension between native Africans and European interlopers, as well as the life-and-death drama at hand—had an acceptable ending. After a heart-pounding stand off, the crowd "dispersed to their homesteads and the girls were spared."

It is important to bear in mind that no single culture or set of religious rituals can be used to summarize the Sudanese of the past century. They constitute a wonderful tapestry of peoples who have brought together tribal influences from different parts of Africa as well as customs from the Arab world and, to a small degree, from Europe.

VILLAGE AND TOWN LIFE

You can see villages of round, thatch-roofed huts in certain parts of the country; rectangular, flat-roofed dwellings in others. Some of the grass-thatched roofs reach almost to the ground, giving the hut a beehive appearance. For siding materials, natives use stones, wood, and mud bricks and plaster.

Most residents of Sudan's cities live in small homes and apartments. In poor areas of a city, the type of housing ranges from

Village in the Mongolla Area, Eastern Equatoria Province, c. 1910

This area is in the southernmost region of the Sudan. It is fairly isolated from the rest of the Sudan by vast swamps to the north and rain forests to the south. Dense jungle-like vegetation covers much of the region. The various peoples who live here practice traditional African religions.

The Azande are the largest ethnic group in the area. This photograph is probably of an Azande village. The Azande are totemic; that is, their society is based on a clan structure with their religion being a worship of ancestors. Polygamy is practiced, with "nobles" having so many wives that it is difficult for younger men to marry. Marriage is contracted by the gift of about 20 spears from the bridegroom to the family of the bride. Girls are married very young—sometimes affianced a few hours after birth.

This photograph was taken by Elizabeth Ness (1880–1962), the first woman Council member of the Royal Geographical Society. She described her extensive travels in her autobiography Ten Thousand Miles in Two Continents *(1929).*

Nuba Women Dancing, 1904 *These dancing Nuba women are from the Tegale area of the Kordofan. The apron, or "sporran," worn by these women is made from twine. All "sporran" follow the same general pattern—a rope waistband bound together with brass rings and a knotted string flap into which have been worked small shells and red, white, and black beads. The only skilled craft practiced by Nuba women is pottery making, with each tribe making a specialty of certain sizes or shapes of pots and bowls.*

huts to tents. Some tribes continue to live, as they have for centuries, under the authority of a chief or "king." To a large extent, they live "from hand to mouth." In many ways, they have been oblivious to the changes and crises that have occurred in the national government since the coming and going of the British.

Certain native groups allow men to have more than one wife; others are monogamous (one-man, one-woman marriages). Among many Sudanese peoples, a bride literally is sold by her parents for either money or livestock. In some cases, the husband must agree to work for the bride's father a certain number of days each year. If a man has more than one wife, each wife might be given a separate hut in the village.

Different tribes have different customs regarding the roles of men and women. Among some peoples, we find both men and women working in crop fields; in others, only men work the fields—or, perhaps, women work the fields close to the village while men farm the lands further away. There might be other seemingly odd divisions in herding and caring for livestock: men tending the cows and goats, for example, while women tend the swine and fowl. In some tribes, certain foods are "taboo," forbidden.

A COMPLEX NATION

Differences in languages, religions, races, and other considerations have resulted in a very complex nation. Though rich in diversity, the people of Sudan live amid certain common, complicated sectional tensions that began hundreds of years ago. Rather than being erased by time, these stresses have grown more complicated with the coming of independence.

Apart from the ongoing civil strife in the south, Sudan in recent years has been plagued by drought, famine, and rampant disease. It also has come under world scrutiny, not only for the tragic human conditions within the country, but for alleged involvement in international terrorism.

Many of modern Sudan's problems were predictable, given the nature of its ethnic divisions and its undeveloped agriculture and industry at the time of independence. Other woes, however, are difficult for outside observers to understand.

Dinka Hut, 1930 *Dinka buildings can last for well over ten years. This is remarkable in a country where termites threaten timber.*

Dinka sleeping huts are built on stilts. This photograph was taken during the dry season (December to April). Wood and mud are used for the walls which are about four feet high. A thatched roof, completed separately, is then placed upon the completed wall. Cattle barns are four times the size of sleeping huts and are never built on stilts.

11

Sudan Today

Despite independence, life in many African nations has changed little since the mid-20th century. Certain areas have seen modest improvements in living conditions, education, health, employment, and transportation. Often these advances have been horribly offset by civil wars costing tens and hundreds of thousands of human casualties. Governments are fragile; attempts at democracy have been problematic. But daily routines for many African citizens, especially rural dwellers, continue much the same as in the days of their ancestors. So it is in Sudan.

Farming and Industry

Only 5 percent of the country is "arable," or suitable for planting crops. Yet, about 80 percent of Sudan's people make their living as farmers, working small fields mainly with hand tools. Their first objective is to grow enough to feed their families, rather than for market.

For producing exports, the government owns large tracts of land, irrigated by the Nile and worked by tenant farmers. Cotton is Sudan's primary export crop. The country also is known for its sorghum, millet (grain harvested from a type of grass), barley, sesame, sugar, citrus fruit, and gum arabic production. Coffee, ebony, rubber, banana, and other types of trees and shrubs are found in the southern rainforests.

Administrative Divisions of Sudan, 1991.

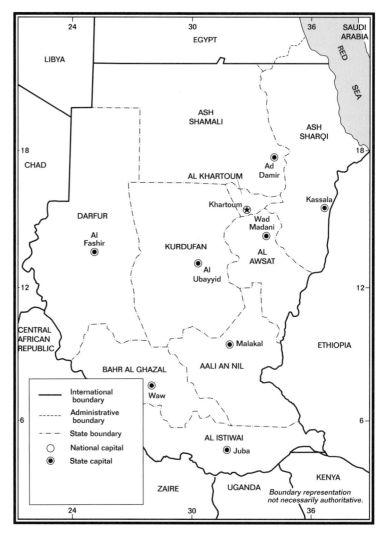

A fraction of the Sudanese, especially in the desert areas, are wandering herders, moving from place to place to find pastures and water for their livestock. They keep cattle, goats, sheep, donkeys and horses, chickens, and dogs. In certain parts of the country we find camels and hogs. In the northern deserts, camel trading has been an important livelihood for some tribes from ancient to modern times. Actually, for many of the rural tribes, livestock is the most meaningful measure of "wealth." Barter (trading), rather than purchasing goods with money, remains commonplace among many agricultural people.

About 10–15 percent of the people are industrial workers. The Ghezira region south of Khartoum is the country's industrial center; other factories are found on the Red Sea coast, especially around Port Sudan. Major industries are textiles and shoemaking, cotton ginning, cement making, and food processing. The Sudanese mine copper, manganese, chromium, lead, gypsum, iron, and other minerals. As with large-scale agriculture, the government runs most of Sudan's industrial operations, although during the 1990s it sold some of its industries to private interests.

A western petroleum company discovered oil in southern Sudan in 1978. Civil warfare in the region, however, has prevented the country from developing oil as a major export. Sudan has an estimated 300 million barrels of crude oil reserves but has to import about four-fifths of the oil its own people consume. Petroleum is, in fact, one of Sudan's primary import items.

In Port Sudan the dockyards offer important work. Along the Red Sea coast, fishing provides a living for some inhabitants. The Nile also is noted for its fishing. (Nile perch can grow as large as an adult man!)

PULSE OF THE PEOPLE

Health care in Sudan is poor, by American standards. Life expectancy is about 55 years. There is an average of only one doctor for every 10,000 people. Infant mortality averages almost 8 percent.

About 175,000 vehicles exist in the country, including passenger cars, buses, and trucks. Fewer than 1 percent of the citizens own a vehicle. You won't be traveling on many paved roads—practically none, once you leave the main northern thoroughfares. The principal paved highway connects Khartoum and Port Sudan; it was completed in 1980. Sudan's poor highway system is cited as a significant stumbling block to commercial progress.

Rail transport thus becomes very important. Sudan has about 3,000 miles of railroads in the government's official Sudan Railway system. Rail lines were built in the northern desert, from Egypt and the Red Sea coast to Khartoum, in the late 1800s and early 1900s. The governing powers have been in little hurry, though, to extend rail transport into southern Sudan.

Sudan's location makes it a natural hub for travel from one region of Africa to another. Not surprisingly, 11 Sudanese airports operate with regular flight schedules. Compared to citizens in western countries, however, the Sudanese are not "well-connected." Only five daily public newspapers are published. There is one telephone, on the average, for approximately every 400 people and one television set for about every 10 people.

What do they do for recreation, you may be wondering. Basically, they do what Americans did until the advent of modern media and diversions: They enjoy the company of family and friends. Those who are gifted with their hands make beautiful crafts much like those fashioned by their ancestors. The country's one significant sport is soccer; as in other African countries, it is quite popular in Sudan.

Arabic, as we've seen, is Sudan's official language and is spoken by more than half the population. In the south, English is used widely in government administration and commerce, although most people in that area speak the native languages of their ancestors. More than 100 languages are spoken throughout the country.

Only about half the people attend school and learn to read and write. Six years of public elementary school education are offered. After that, children may go on to three- or four-year secondary schools where they are trained for business, teaching, or modern farming. One of the three-year secondary school programs is college preparatory, but only 3 percent of the population attends college. Sudan has five universities.

Some Sudanese dress much the same as in western countries; others wear traditional clothing. Women in the cities usually wear a head-to-foot covering called a "taub" over their ordinary clothes. Some of the men wear a "jallabiyah," a type of flowing robe; a "taqiyah," or skullcap; and an "imamah," or white turban. In the remote, arid areas, though, hot weather compels farmers to wear only scant clothing. It is only natural that in a largely desert nation like Sudan, sandals are the standard type of shoes.

What is the food like? Not all Sudanese are vegetarians, but they eat much less meat than Americans. The mealtime staple

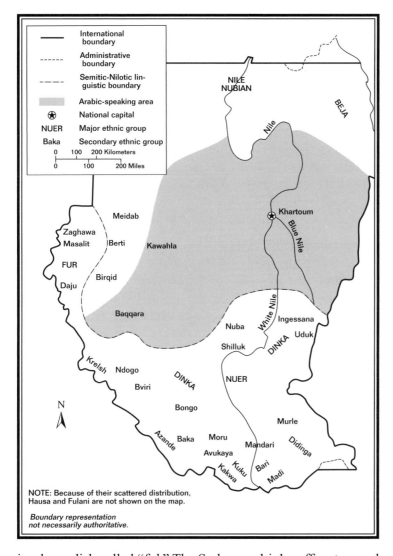

Principle Ethnolinguistic Groups, 1991.

Legend:
- International boundary
- Administrative boundary
- Semitic-Nilotic linguistic boundary
- Arabic-speaking area
- ★ National capital
- **NUER** Major ethnic group
- Baka Secondary ethnic group

0   100   200 Kilometers
0   100   200 Miles

NOTE: Because of their scattered distribution, Hausa and Fulani are not shown on the map.

Boundary representation not necessarily authoritative.

is a bean dish called "ful." The Sudanese drink coffee, tea, and a hibiscus drink called "karkadai."

The Future: A Question Mark

As we've seen in this book, a conspiracy of factors beyond geography have for thousands of years separated the people of the north from those of the south. Great Britain, when it became involved in governing the country, recognized these serious, long-standing divisions. The English decided the simplest way to deal with them would be to create northern and southern divisions of government administration.

When Sudan became independent in 1956, northern Arabs replaced British government officials in southern Sudan, prompting an immediate threat of rebellion in the south. Soon enough, as we've seen, the south was embroiled in civil war. As in so many new African nations, regional/racial/ethnic tensions continue to impede efforts toward unity and progress today.

Under the Al-Bashir regime, Sudan has become increasingly alienated from western countries like the United States and from certain Arab nations. Sudan was one of the few countries to support Iraq during the 1991 Gulf War. "Isolationism" has come to describe the modern Khartoum government.

Sudan in recent years has come under world criticism for its treatment of certain ethnic peoples and for possibly sheltering international terrorist groups. The government was accused of "ethnic cleansing" against the Nuba in southern Sudan in 1993. Two years later Sudanese terrorists were accused of trying to assassinate Hosni Mubarak, the president of Egypt. In 1998 U.S. embassies in Tanzania and Kenya were bombed by terrorists. More than 200 people died in the bombings, including 12 Americans. The United States retaliated with missile attacks on suspected terrorist bases in Sudan and Afghanistan.

Time alone will tell what happens next in the history of what has been called the "unstable state" of Sudan. For the moment, it appears democracy (the parliament system) has failed. As an impoverished society under an authoritarian government, Sudan appears to be contributing little as a member of the global community. Yet, its geographic location—the crossroads between Arab and African worlds—ensures Sudan an important place in the overall progress of the newly independent continent. The winds of development may change. We can hope that in Sudan, they change for the better.

CHRONOLOGY

Before 13,000 B.C.	First humans lived in what is modern-day Sudan.
1000 B.C.	The Kush kingdom in northern Sudan emerges as a major power of the middle Nile.
6th century A.D.	European missionaries introduce Christianity along the Nile in Nubia (northern Sudan/southern Egypt).
7th century	Muslims from Arabia invade Egypt and Nubia.
1250	Mamluk slaves rise to power in Egypt and begin raiding into Nubia.
16th century	Ottoman Turks overrun Egypt.
Circa 1500–1800	The Funj kingdom of the Blue Nile controls the Sudan region.
1805	The Ottoman Turks appoint Muhammad Ali "pasha," or governor, of Egypt.
1820–21	Muhammad Ali sets up a Turkish/Egyptian government in Khartoum.
1863	Ismail Pasha is appointed viceroy of Egypt and Sudan; brings European influences and resources into the Nile valley.
1869	Ismail Pasha sends English explorer Samuel White Baker up the Nile to quash the slave trade. Baker establishes the Sudan province of Equatoria and becomes its governor.
1877	English soldier Charles George Gordon is named governor-general of Sudan.
1881	Muhammad Ahmad proclaims himself the "Mahdi." His armies begin overrunning the middle Nile region.
1885	Mahdist forces capture Khartoum and slaughter Gordon and his defending garrison; several months later, the Mahdi dies and is succeeded by his deputy, the Khalifah.
1896–99	Herbert Kitchener's Anglo-Egyptian forces reconquer Sudan from the Mahdists.
1899	British and Egyptian leaders form a "condominium" to oversee Sudan.
1924	Sudan Governor-General Sir Lee Stack is assassinated.
1948	A new Legislative Assembly replaces the condominium's Executive Council to govern Sudan.
1953	A trial period of self-government begins in Sudan.
January 1, 1956	The Republic of the Sudan becomes an independent nation.

CHRONOLOGY

1958	Army leaders take control of the government.
1964–65	The army returns government control to an elective system.
1969	Army Col. Jaafar an Nimeiri seizes power.
1972	Southern rebel forces are granted a measure of autonomy, temporarily ending years of civil war in that region of Sudan.
1985	Nimeiri is ousted in another military coup.
1988	Col. Umar Hassan Ahmad al-Bashir takes control; his regime continues to the present time.
1998	U.S. embassies in Tanzania and Kenya are bombed, with heavy casualties; the terrorists responsible for the bombings are believed to have been based in Sudan and Afghanistan.

WORLD WITHOUT END

DEIRDRE SHIELDS

ONE SUMMER'S DAY in 1830, a group of Englishmen met in London and decided to start a learned society to promote "that most important and entertaining branch of knowledge—Geography," and the Royal Geographical Society (RGS) was born.

The society was formed by the Raleigh Travellers' Club, an exclusive dining club, whose members met over exotic meals to swap tales of their travels. Members included Lord Broughton, who had travelled with the poet Byron, and John Barrow, who had worked in the iron foundries of Liverpool before becoming a force in the British Admiralty.

From the start, the Royal Geographical Society led the world in exploration, acting as patron and inspiration for the great expeditions to Africa, the Poles, and the Northwest Passage, that elusive sea connection between the Atlantic and Pacific. In the scramble to map the world, the society embodied the spirit of the age: that English exploration was a form of benign conquest.

The society's gold medal awards for feats of exploration read like a Who's Who of famous explorers, among them David Livingstone, for his 1855 explorations in Africa; the American explorer Robert Peary, for his 1898 discovery of the "northern termination of the Greenland ice"; Captain Robert Scott, the first Englishman to reach the South Pole, in 1912; and on and on.

Today the society's headquarters, housed in a red-brick Victorian lodge in South Kensington, still has the effect of a gentleman's club, with courteous staff, polished wood floors, and fine paintings.

AFTERWORD

The building archives the world's most important collection of private exploration papers, maps, documents, and artefacts. Among the RGS's treasures are the hats Livingstone and Henry Morton Stanley wore at their famous meeting ("Dr. Livingstone, I presume?") at Ujiji in 1871, and the chair the dying Livingstone was carried on during his final days in Zambia. The collection also includes models of expedition ships, paintings, dug-out canoes, polar equipment, and Charles Darwin's pocket sextant.

The library's 500,000 images cover the great moments of exploration. Here is Edmund Hillary's shot of Sherpa Tenzing standing on Everest. Here is Captain Lawrence Oates, who deliberately walked out of his tent in a blizzard to his death because his illness threatened to delay Captain Scott's party. Here, too is the American Museum of Natural History's 1920 expedition across the Gobi Desert in dusty convoy (the first to drive motorised vehicles across a desert).

The day I visited, curator Francis Herbert was trying to find maps for five different groups of adventurers at the same time from the largest private map collection in the world. Among the 900,000 items are maps dating to 1482 and ones showing the geology of the moon and thickness of ice in Antarctica, star atlases, and "secret" topographic maps from the former Soviet Union.

The mountaineer John Hunt pitched a type of base camp in a room at the RGS when he organised the 1953 Everest expedition that put Hillary and Tenzing on top of the world. "The society was my base, and source of my encouragement," said the late Lord Hunt, who noted that the nature of that work is different today from what it was when he was the society's president from 1976 to 1980. "When I was involved, there was still a lot of genuine territorial exploration to be done. Now, virtually every important corner—of the land surface, at any rate—has been discovered, and exploration has become more a matter of detail, filling in the big picture."

The RGS has shifted from filling in blanks on maps to providing a lead for the new kind of exploration, under the banner of geography: "I see exploration not so much as a question of 'what' and 'where' anymore, but 'why' and 'how': How does the earth work, the environment function, and how do we manage our resources sustainably?" says the society's director, Dr. Rita Gardner. "Our role today is to answer such questions at the senior level of scientific research," Gardner continues, "through our big, multidisciplinary expeditions, through the smaller expeditions we support and encourage, and by advancing the subject of geography, advising governments, and encouraging wider public understanding. Geography is the subject of the 21st century because it embraces everything—peoples, cultures, landscapes, environments—and pulls them all together."

The society occupies a unique position in world-class exploration. To be invited to speak at the RGS is still regarded as an accolade, the ultimate seal of approval of Swan, who in 1989 became the first person to walk to both the North and South Poles, and who says, "The hairs still stand on the back of my neck when I think about the first time I spoke at the RGS. It was the greatest honour."

The RGS set Swan on the path of his career as an explorer, assisting him with a 1979 expedition retracing Scott's journey to the South Pole. "I was a Mr. Nobody, trying to raise seven million dollars, and getting nowhere," says Swan. "The RGS didn't tell me I was mad—they gave me access to Scott's private papers. From those, I found fifty sponsors who had supported Scott, and persuaded them to fund me. On the basis of a photograph I found of one of his chaps sitting on a box of 'Shell Spirit,' I got Shell to sponsor the fuel for my ship."

The name "Royal Geographical Society" continues to open doors. Although the society's actual membership—some 12,600 "fellows," as they are called—is small, the organisation offers an incomparable network of people, experience, and expertise. This is seen in the work of the Expeditionary Advisory Centre. The EAC was established in 1980 to provide a focus for would-be explorers. If you want to know how to raise sponsorship, handle snakes safely, or find a mechanic for your trip across the Sahara, the EAC can help. Based in Lord Hunt's old Everest office, the EAC funds some 50 small expeditions a year and offers practical training and advice to hundreds more. Its safety tips range from the pragmatic—"In subzero temperatures, metal spectacle frames can cause frostbite (as can earrings and nose-rings)"—to the unnerving—"Remember: A decapitated snake head can still bite."

The EAC is unique, since it is the only centre in the world that helps small-team, low-budget expeditions, thus keeping the amateur—in the best sense of the word—tradition of exploration alive.

AFTERWORD

"The U.K. still sends out more small expeditions per capita than any other country," says Dr. John Hemming, director of the RGS from 1975 to 1996. During his tenure, Hemming witnessed the growth in exploration-travel. "In the 1960s we'd be dealing with 30 to 40 expeditions a year. By 1997 it was 120, but the quality hadn't gone down—it had gone up. It's a boom time for exploration, and the RGS is right at the heart of it."

While the EAC helps adventure-travellers, it concentrates its funding on scientific field research projects, mostly at the university level. Current projects range from studying the effect of the pet trade on Madagscar's chameleons, to mapping uncharted terrain in the south Ecuadorian cloud forest. Jen Hurst is a typical "graduate" of the EAC. With two fellow Oxford students, she received EAC technical training, support, and a $2,000 grant to do biological surveys in the Kyabobo Range, a new national park in Ghana.

"The RGS's criteria for funding are very strict," says Hurst. "They put you through a real grilling, once you've made your application. They're very tough on safety, and very keen on working alongside people from the host country. The first thing they wanted to be sure of was whether we would involve local students. They're the leaders of good practice in the research field."

When Hurst and her colleagues returned from Ghana in 1994, they presented a case study of their work at an EAC seminar. Their talk prompted a $15,000 award from the BP oil company for them to set up a registered charity, the Kyabobo Conservation Project, to ensure that work in the park continues, and that followup ideas for community-based conservation, social, and education projects are developed. "It's been a great experience, and crucial to the careers we hope to make in environmental work," says Hurst. "And it all started through the RGS."

The RGS is rich in prestige but it is not particularly wealthy in financial terms. Compared to the National Geographic Society in the U.S., the RGS is a pauper. However, bolstered by sponsorship from such companies as British Airways and Discovery Channel Europe, the RGS remains one of Britain's largest organisers of geographical field research overseas.

The ten major projects the society has undertaken over the last 20 or so years have spanned the world, from Pakistan and Oman to Brunei and Australia. The scope is large—hundreds of people are currently working in the field and the emphasis is multidisciplinary, with the aim to break down traditional barriers, not only among the different strands of science but also among nations. This is exploration as The Big Picture, preparing blueprints for governments around the globe to work on. For example, the 1977 Mulu (Sarawak) expedition to Borneo was credited with kick-starting the international concern for tropical rain forests.

The society's three current projects include water and soil erosion studies in Nepal, sustainable land use in Jordan, and a study of the Mascarene Plateau in the western Indian Ocean, to develop ideas on how best to conserve ocean resources in the future.

Projects adhere to a strict code of procedure. "The society works only at the invitation of host governments and in close co-operation with local people," explains Winser. "The findings are published in the host countries first, so they can get the benefit. Ours are long-term projects, looking at processes and trends, adding to the sum of existing knowledge, which is what exploration is about."

Exploration has never been more fashionable in England. More people are travelling adventurously on their own account, and the RGS's increasingly younger membership (the average age has dropped in the last 20 years from over 45 to the early 30s) is exploration-literate and able to make the fine distinctions between adventure / extreme / expedition / scientific travel.

Rebecca Stephens, who in 1993 became the first British woman to summit Everest, says she "pops along on Monday evenings to listen to the lectures." These occasions are sociable, informal affairs, where people find themselves talking to such luminaries as explorer Sir Wilfred Thesiger, who attended Haile Selassie's coronation in Ethiopia in 1930, or David Puttnam, who produced the film *Chariots of Fire* and is a vice president of the RGS. Shortly before his death, Lord Hunt was spotted in deep conversation with the singer George Michael.

Summing up the society's enduring appeal, Shane Winser says, "The Royal Geographical Society is synonymous with exploration, which is seen as something brave and exciting. In a sometimes dull, depressing world, the Royal Geographical Society offers a spirit of adventure people are always attracted to."

FURTHER READING

Abbas, Mekki. *The Sudan Question: The Dispute Over the Anglo-Egyptian Condominium, 1884–1951*. New York: Frederick A. Praeger, Inc., Publishers, 1952.

Anderson, G. Norman. *Sudan in Crisis: The Failure of Democracy*. Gainesville, Fla.: University Press of Florida, 1999.

Barbour, K.M. *The Republic of the Sudan: A Regional Geography*. London: University of London Press Ltd, 1961.

Fairservis, Walter A., Jr. *The Ancient Kingdoms of the Nile*. New York: The New American Library, Inc., 1962.

Gifford, Prosser, and William Roger Louis, editors. *France and Britain in Africa: Imperial Rivalry and Colonial Rule*. New Haven, Conn.: Yale University Press, 1971.

Henderson, K.D.D. *Sudan Republic*. New York: Frederick A. Praeger, Inc., Publishers, 1965.

Metz, Helen Chapin, editor. *Sudan: A Country Study*, Fourth Edition. Federal Research Division, Library of Congress, 1992.

Murdock, George Peter. *Africa: Its Peoples and Their Culture History*. New York: McGraw-Hill Book Company, 1959.

Oliver, Roland, and Fage, J.D. *A Short History of Africa*. Harmondsworth, Middlesex, England: Penguin Books Ltd., 1970.

Packenham, Thomas. *The Scramble for Africa: 1876–1912*. New York: Random House, 1991.

Toniolo, Eilias, and Hill, Richard, editors. *The Opening of the Nile Basin: Writings by Members of the Catholic Mission to Central Africa on the Geography and Ethnography of the Sudan, 1842–1881*. New York: Harper & Row Publishers, Inc. 1975.

Woodward, Peter. *Sudan, 1898–1989: The Unstable State*. Boulder, Colo.: Lynne Rienner Publishers, Inc., 1990.

ABOUT THE AUTHORS

Dr. Richard E. Leakey is a distinguished paleo-anthropologist and conservationist. He is chairman of the Wildlife Clubs of Kenya Association and the Foundation for the Research into the Origins of Man. He presented the BBC-TV series *The Making of Mankind* (1981) and wrote the accompanying book. His other publications include *People of the Lake* (1979) and *One Life* (1984). Richard Leakey, along with his famous parents, Louis and Mary, was named by *Time* magazine as one of the greatest minds of the twentieth century.

Daniel E. Harmon is an editor and writer living in Spartanburg, South Carolina. The author of several books on history, he has contributed historical and cultural articles to *The New York Times, Music Journal, Nautilus,* and many other periodicals. He is the managing editor of *Sandlapper: The Magazine of South Carolina* and editor of *The Lawyer's PC* newsletter.

Deirdre Shields is the author of many articles dealing with contemporary life in Great Britain. Her essays have appeared in *The Times, The Daily Telegraph, Harpers & Queen*, and *The Field*.

INDEX

Numerals in italics indicate a photograph of the subject mentioned.